TRUTH BLINDNESS

THE TRUE BOOK OF LIFE

GENE JUSTICE

Only One Publishing

TRUTH BLINDNESS
The True Book of Life
All Rights Reserved.
Copyright © 2020 Gene Justice
v6.0 r1.1

The opinions expressed in this manuscript are solely the opinions of the author and do not represent the opinions or thoughts of the publisher. The author has represented and warranted full ownership and/or legal right to publish all the materials in this book.

This book may not be reproduced, transmitted, or stored in whole or in part by any means, including graphic, electronic, or mechanical without the express written consent of the publisher except in the case of brief quotations embodied in critical articles and reviews.

Only One Publishing

Paperback ISBN: 978-0-578-22308-7
Hardback ISBN: 978-0-578-22309-4

PRINTED IN THE UNITED STATES OF AMERICA

This book was written for, and is dedicated to my Lord God. Thank you so much for all you do and for enriching my life with your infinite love.

SPECIAL THANKS

I would like to express my sincerest thanks to my wife Deloris and my aunt Janie for all their support and help. For the hours they spent proof reading, their patience, and love.

I would also like to thank my family and friends for sticking with me throughout my life, I love you each and everyone.

TABLE OF CONTENTS

Introduction i
1. The Beginning 1
2. Characteristics of the Creator 3
3. The Law of Reason 12
4. The Law of Creation 21
5. Speaking on Gods Behalf.................. 27
6. The Beginning of God Myths 29
7. The Revealing of God Myths............. 34
8. Spoken Word of God 37
9. Inspired Word of God 50
10. Creation Myths Revealed 54
11. Genesis Creation................................ 55
12. The Big Bang Myth.............................. 60
13. The Evolution Myth 86
14. The Fossil Record Myth 92
15. Similarity Myth 94
16. Mutation Myth 96
17. Spontaneous Generation Myth 98
18. The Intelligence Behind DNA 101
19. God Myths Continued....................... 104

20. The One True God 113
21. New Testament Contradictions 115
22. The Worshipping of Jesus 122
23. The Trinity Myth 125
24. Revealing the Antichrist 129
25. This Is What We Do Know 139
26. The Largest Hoax in the History of the World 141
27. Free Will 144
28. Gods Will 149
29. Your Purpose 154
30. Love – Joy – Hope and Suicide 156
31. Prayer 160
32. Life After Death 163
33. The Meaning of Life 167
34. Dealing with Death 169
35. Happiness 171
36. Children Beware 173
37. A World Without Religion 181
38. Traditions and Rituals 185
39. Thoughts and Inspiration 188
40. In Closing 194

INTRODUCTION

Often enforced by TRADITIONS and PERSECUTION over a period of time, TRUTH BLINDNESS occurs when myths and falsehoods become accepted as absolute truth.

WARNING: This book deals with Real Life Truths, many things in life that you thought were true will be turned upside down. Because we live in a matrix of lies and deception, careful consideration should be taken before reading as such truths CAN'T BE UNDONE.

For the **TRUTH SEEKERS** and those yearning for **LIFE'S ANSWERS**, these pages will become your companion.

"So many of our young children are looking for **REAL LIFE ANSWERS**, if you have children or grandchildren, this book may be the best gift you could give them"

Within the pages of this book I'll be sharing **THE TRUTH** behind life's most perplexing and meaningful issues, such as: Religion, Science, your Purpose in Life, and The Meaning of Life. I'll also be revealing The Antichrist, and The Biggest Hoax Ever, plus much more.

To avoid confusion and misinterpretations, great strides were taken to eliminate wasted words, thus you won't find a whole chapter dedicated to something that can be explained with a couple sentences.

You will find this book tackles the tough questions head on and straight to the point, giving you answers that are based on facts and truth.

The first four chapters are science and evidence driven, and may start out a bit slow for some. However, it was important to build a solid and credible foundation, as there are many **NAYSAYERS** and those that have **TRUTH BLINDNESS**.

When discerning between Truth and Fabrication, reliable evidence is an essential ingredient. Therefore, expert proof and opinions are shared throughout these pages to defend the revealing truths.

In the past there have been many books written on the subject of creation and life, but the most highly regarded of all are the ancient writings found within the Bible, Torah, and the Quran.

Even though these ancient writings date back thousands of years, they are more popular today than when they were written. In addition, these writings are so intertwined within our society that many of their traditions are still in existence to this day.

Because these ancient writings have had such an amazing impact, we'll be discussing them further. More importantly we'll be searching them for **TRUTH**.

"BEWARE OF TRADITION AND EGO, THEY HATE CHANGE AND TRUTH"

To grasp the complete message within this book, PLEASE take the time to read it cover to cover, starting from The Beginning. After reading, if you have any questions or comments, please visit my website at **TRUTHBLINDNESS.COM**, submit your question(s) or comments and I'll do my best to clarify, and answer as many questions as possible.

"<u>**ANY DEVIATION** from that which is written, is not of this book</u>"

Chapter 1

THE BEGINNING

> In the beginning was the CREATOR, before anything else existed, the CREATOR was.

In the following pages concrete evidence will be given for the existence of The Creator, but for right now one should understand the Creator is INFINITE, as such the Creator can't be defined in absoluteness, nor minimized by equation or formula.

Einstein in his book, The World As I See It, wrote about the mysteries of life and creation:

"A knowledge of the existence of something we cannot penetrate .... of the manifestations of the profoundest reason and the most radiant beauty.......... which are only accessible to our reason in their most elementary forms."

Einstein understood trying to define something that was truly infinite was beyond full understanding, and that the best we could possible hope for would be to understand tiny pieces of the whole.

As such, our knowledge of the Creator is also limited, however; there are certain characteristics that the Creator has revealed, so let's begin by taking a closer look at what we do know.

Chapter 2

CHARACTERISTICS OF THE CREATOR

In physics, one of most basic laws of science is the Law of Conservation, which states: *Energy can be neither created nor be destroyed.*

> This would mean that some type of energy has ALWAYS EXISTED.

Therefore, because the Creator has always existed, we must conclude that one characteristic of the Creator is ENERGY.

Although we don't know the exact type of energy the Creator possesses, we do know it's PURE ENERGY, NON-ATOMIC, INFINITE, and what some may refer to as SPIRIT.

This SPIRIT/ENERGY has always existed!

Socrates said: *"Energy, or soul, is separate from matter, and that the universe is made of energy – pure energy which was there before man and other material things like the earth came along"*

It would seem Socrates was on the right track, however; we now know that even matter when it's broken down to its smallest scales, "atoms and subatomic particles" matter is also energy.

EVERYONE and EVERYTHING is made of energy.

There's atomic energy, which is anything that is made up of atoms or have come from atoms. Then there's the PURE/SPIRIT energy of the Creator, which IS NOT MADE UP OF ATOMS, and has always existed.

For a better understanding of pure/spirit energy we need to look back prior to what science refers to as the Big Bang, as science claims it was only after the Big Bang that atoms were created.

We'll be discussing the Big Bang in more details later, but for now we'll concur with science that prior to the Big Bang there were no atoms; however, there was pure energy.

{It's important for one to understand that PURE/SPIRIT energy is not atomic based, and that the Creator existed before atoms or anything else}

PURE/SPIRIT ENERGY is just one infinite characteristic of the Creator, so let's continue.

In addition to energy not being created or destroyed the LAW OF CONSERVATION ALSO STATES: "ENERGY CAN CHANGE FROM ONE FORM TO ANOTHER."

Therefore, if energy can change from one form to another, and the Creator possesses infinite amounts of pure energy, it's only logical to believe another characteristic of the Creator would be the ability to CHANGE OR CREATE DIFFERENT FORMS.

Science has concluded that only 4.9% of the universe is ordinary matter, things such as atoms, stars, planets, and anything visible. As for the other 95% of the universe, it's still unknown to science. It is thought to be made up of Dark Matter and Dark Energy however, both are only hypothetical.

It should come as no surprise that with an infinite amount of pure energy, the Creator could easily create such a small amount of ordinary matter, and hence the universe and everything in it.

> "One must understand that the Creator has always existed, and everything beyond the Creator forward has been created"

Let's evaluate another characteristic of the Creator; Intelligence.

According to an estimate made by engineers at Washington University, there are around 100 trillion atoms in a typical human cell, and the human body has trillions of cells. Each atom is a miniature power source, thus we ourselves are truly **ENERGY BEINGS**.

As energy beings, it's energy that gives us the ability to think and to reason, as billions of nerve cells communicate with each other through electrical impulses.

One may argue that intelligence is only possible because of the brain; however, the brain is only the conduit for our human bodies, without electrical impulses the brain doesn't function.

Let's consider the jellyfish for a moment, it's said they are the oldest multi-organ animal known, and they have roamed the seas for 500 – 700 million years. Jellyfish hunt, they breed, they swim, and they are very capable of defending themselves, however; what makes them such amazing animals is that they have no brain.

Instead of a brain, jellyfish survive by using a nerve net that transmits electrical impulses to other nerve cells. Once again, it should be made clear that **LIFE** and **INTELLIGENCE** is all about **ENERGY**.

> "If our own intelligence is based on energy, it's only logical to believe that the Creator whose energy is pure and infinite, would also possess intelligence"

"This most beautiful system of the sun, planets, and comets, could only proceed from the counsel and dominion of an intelligent Being......Sir Isaac Newton"

Einstein said: *"Everyone who is seriously involved in the pursuit of science becomes convinced that a spirit is manifest in the laws of the Universe - a spirit vastly superior to that of man, and one in the face of which we with our modest powers must feel humble"*

Max Planck, the father of quantum physics was a theoretical physicist whose work on quantum theory won him the Nobel Prize. Planck said in 1944:

"As a man who has devoted his whole life to the most clear headed science, to the study of matter, I can

tell you as a result of my research about atoms this much: There is no matter as such. All matter originates and exists only by virtue of a force which brings the particle of an atom to vibration and holds this most minute solar system of the atom together. We must assume behind this force the existence of a conscious and intelligent mind. This mind is the matrix of all matter"

Also, according to John Hagelin, a quantum physicist with a PhD from Harvard: *"Consciousness is universal, and the properties of the Unified Field is the most concentrated field of intelligence in nature, nonmaterial, dynamic, self-aware intelligence"* Hagelin further reports that consciousness is NOT created by the brain, but fundamental in nature."

"THE CREATOR IS THE SOURCE OF ALL ENERGY, CONTROLLING AND DIRECTING IT AT WILL"

Energy is the universal component of **LIFE**, and **ALL INTELLIGENCE**.

In nature all the images of energy that you see, that we are, has been formed by the Creator.

Let's now look at another characteristic that we know the Creator possesses; THE POWER/ENERGY/SPIRIT OF LOVE.

Love is good, love is peace, love is understanding, love is joy, love is merciful, love is forgiveness, love is truth, love is just, love is hope, love is compassion, and PURE LOVE IS PERFECT. PURE LOVE is the essence of PURE ENERGY, and there is no greater power.

Because the Creator possesses infinite amounts of pure energy, there's no doubt the Creator also possesses infinite amounts of pure love.

> "WE ARE ALL ENERGY FORMS, as such we possess consciousness, intelligence, emotions, and free will, all of which the Creator has freely given"

"KNOW THIS ABOVE ALL THINGS, LOVE IS THE THREAD THAT BINDS US TO THE CREATOR, FOR IT WAS OUT OF LOVE THAT WE WERE CREATED"

Love is the pathway to our Creator, we connect and communicate through love, the purer your love, the better the connection.

Chapter 3

THE LAW OF REASON

The Law of Reason states: For everything that happens, there is a reason.

REASON: a cause, explanation, or justification for an action or event.

Over the centuries humankind has made many discoveries, things once unimaginable are now a reality, however, there are still many mysteries that are yet beyond our current understanding; hence sometimes reason may still elude us.

Below are a few examples of the Law of Reason at work:

A motorist rams his vehicle into another car, some consider this an accident, and accidents just happen, this is UNTRUE. There is always a reason for an accident, they don't JUST HAPPEN.

In this case the driver took his eyes off the road, he may have been drinking, texting, or eating, it doesn't really matter, he wasn't concentrating on his driving, and that is the reason for the wreck.

A skydivers parachute fails to open, the reason......bad packing.

A swimmer drowns, the reason..... cramps.

A tire goes flat; the reason could have been a defected tire, a puncture, wear, etc. Tires don't just deflate without a reason, nothing happens without a reason.

In 1968, a scientist at 3M in the United States, Dr. Spencer Silver, was attempting to develop a super-strong adhesive, instead he unknowingly created a "low-tack", reusable, pressure-sensitive adhesive, what we now refer to as "Post-It Notes". Now some may consider this as being lucky, however, the reason why we have Post-it

Notes is because someone realized a use for it.

We could go on and on with different examples, but the Law of Reason is clear, nothing happens without a reason.

Contrary to what science calls LUCK, the Law of Reason clearly demonstrates that the universe and life itself didn't just happen, and that there is a reason for our existence.

Nothing as complex as the universe and life just pops into existence out of nothingness, that type of thinking is reserved for witch doctors and magicians.

The Law of Reason is just another part of human nature that assures us there is a Creator.

CHOICE AND RISK

A man is riding his motorcycle home from work one evening, as he goes through an intersection another driver runs the red light, and the motorcyclist dies in the crash.

After a careful investigation it was discovered that the driver that ran the red light had been driving while under the influence of alcohol, as such the wreck was attributed to alcohol use. However, a traumatic brain injury is actually what caused the death of the motorcyclist.

Even though there was a clear reason for the death of the motorcyclist, his family still doesn't understand, **WHY DID HE HAVE TO DIE**. I know losing a loved one is never easy, and in cases such as the motorcyclist it's not uncommon for loved ones to ask, **WHY HIM/HER**. Therefore, before we go any further, please allow me to address this question.

To better understand the Law of Reason, and to help the family understand why the motorcyclist died, it's important that we discuss **CHOICE & RISK** briefly.

Let me start off by saying this, the motorcyclist didn't have to die in the wreck, however, because of **CHOICE & RISK** he did.

Every day from the time we wake up until we fall asleep we are making choices, we choose when or if we are getting out of bed, taking a shower, brushing our teeth, having breakfast, what we'll be wearing, etc, and we do this all day.

The choices we make often times become so routine that we no longer even consider the risk involved; it's this type of complacency that puts us in harm's way.

For example: Driving when we are tired, speeding, texting, drinking and eating, not wearing seat belts, etc. Life has enough dangers without us complicating things or making matters worse, for when we do, terrible things are likely to occur.

"We have become so conditioned to making choices that often times we overlook the risks that are involved"

Though we don't dwell on it, we all know of the dangers involved with driving, and as drivers we accept that risk every time we get behind the wheel, the motorcyclist understood this and accepted the risk.

Now let's examine how Choice & Risk played its part in the death of the motorcyclist.

The motorcyclist died from a brain injury, the type of injury that was avoidable had he been wearing a helmet. Let's take it one step further, if the motorcyclist had been driving a car on that day, the risk of him dying in the crash would have been zero.

Choice & Risk is always present, and even though the wreck happened because someone was driving impaired, we can see how the wreck was much worse than it had to be. The choice made by the motorcyclist not to wear a helmet, or drive a car, is really why he died. Every year there are thousands that die simply because they choose not to wear a seatbelt, and bad choices can be deadly!

This example isn't meant to imply the motorcyclist was at fault, only to illustrate the importance that CHOICE & RISK play in our daily lives.

John Doe wins the lottery so how does the Law of Reason apply.

By playing John took a risk, which then created an opportunity that wasn't there prior, simply put, the reason John won was because he played the game.

Games such as the lottery are based on odds, the fact that John's numbers matched was based more upon his ability to take a risk and play the game, than picking the correct numbers, as such had John chose the correct numbers and didn't play the game, he would not have won.

> "Randomness and odds are nothing more than multiple options"

Nothing in life happens without taking some amount of risk. Sam Walton risked opening up his first store, thus Wal-Mart. We all take risks every day; it's a part of life. Usually the larger the risk, the larger the reward, however; it's important for us to take calculated and reasonable risk.

Choice and Risk is a part of life, and when we take calculated risks, it creates opportunities for us that were not there before.

We must not allow our fears to hold us back.

A casino doesn't stay in business because they're lucky, they stay in business because they understand the risk. "Remember the odds in gambling are terrible!!"

There's an old saying that goes; "The harder I work the luckier I get" this is so true, because people that work hard create for themselves more opportunities. Good fortune isn't about luck, it's mostly about hard work, calculated risk, opportunity, and how you apply them.

Lucky charms, astrology, and numerology are nothing but superstition, and bad luck is often an excuse for those that refuse to take responsibility for their bad choices.

Remember the sun shines equally on the good and the bad.

> "Good fortune isn't about dollars and cents, it's about love"

These examples were used because people often confuse games of chance with luck, instead of risk and opportunity. There is also a misconception about winning, as though winning is always a good thing, however, this isn't always true.

Many people that have won the lottery have lost it all, their winnings, their family, friends, and sometimes even their own life. I personally knew a guy that won the lottery that didn't have a dime to his name, he was also an alcoholic. After winning the lottery he was able to buy all the liquor he wanted, and within a short time he drank himself to death, as you can see this wasn't much of a win.

Chapter 4

THE LAW OF CREATION

The Law of Creation states: For every creation, there is a Creator

> "THIS IS THE MOST SIMPLISTIC LAW OF ALL, AS IT IS SELF-EVIDENT"

To prove this Law, one only needs to look around. The television you watch, the bed you sleep in, the car that you drive, and the house that you live in, all of these creations had a creator.

> "The more complex something is, the greater the creativity and intelligence behind it"

A writer creates a book, a builder creates a mall, a playwright creates a play, an artist creates a masterpiece, and a man and a woman creates a child.

"EVERY CREATION STARTS WITH A CREATOR"

When we discuss Creator vs Creation, it prompts that age old question; which came first, the chicken or the egg?

According to the Law of Creation, the chicken would be the creator, and the egg is the offspring/creator.

> The Law of Creation is universal and self-evident in all of nature.

The chicken and the egg scenario isn't as perplexing as it may seem, however, there are certain aspects that was left out of this procreation teaser, such as all chickens don't lay eggs.

Any farmer will confirm only a female chicken "hen" can lay an egg, and the male chicken "rooster" cannot. This may sound silly, but it's a very important part of the puzzle.

In addition, for the hen to produce an offspring it must first mate with a rooster, and although a hen can lay an egg without mating with a rooster, the egg WILL NOT BE FERTILE, thus no offspring will be created.

One can clearly see that the question; "Which came first the chicken or the egg" was lacking some important details. So let's deal with the realities of procreation and ask the correct question;

Which came first, the hen and the rooster, or an egg that wasn't created by a hen or fertilized by a rooster?

As further proof the hen and rooster were first, had the egg been first without a chicken to **NURTURE** it, and keep it warm, it would have never hatched.

Here's another example from a different perspective; which came first, the baby or the parents?

As we all know it takes a man and a woman to create a child, and as any parent can testify, without years of **NURTURING**, no baby can survive on its own.

The parents and chickens are the creators and they came first, the child and the egg is their creation, their offspring. These are the facts, and they are undeniable and irrefutable.

> "The Law of Creation is simplistic, and absolute; for **EVERY CREATION**, there must be a **CREATOR**"

With simple reasoning, we know it's impossible to have creation without a creator, we also know behind every creation there's intelligence.

The Law of Creation is based on the undisputable truth that everything that has ever been created has a creator. This law applies to everything in nature, furthermore, it validates that the universe itself was indeed intelligently created, and leaves no room for speculation.

> "EVERY CREATION STARTS WITH A CREATOR, THIS IS THE NATURE OF ALL THINGS"

> "THE EXISTENCE OF OUR CREATOR IS SELF-EVIDENT"

Many will choose to deny the obvious truth of this law, for vanity runs deep and is blinding.

EINSTEIN: *"When the solution is simple, God is answering."*

Let it be known, the solution is simple, GOD is our CREATOR.

Let us summarize:

Nothing creates nothing, which means there had to be something in the beginning that has always existed.

The Law of Conservation states: "Energy cannot be created or destroyed" therefore, in the beginning there was pure energy, this energy is a characteristic of God.

The Law of Conservation also states: That energy can change forms "this is what we view as matter"

The Law of Reason states: "For everything that happens there is a reason" this means there had to be a reason for the creation of the universe and everything in it.

Finally, the Law of Creation states: "For every creation, there is a creator" this law makes it unquestionably clear that the creation of the universe wasn't happenchance, and further validates that the universe was indeed intelligently created.

Chapter 5

SPEAKING ON GODS BEHALF

Like sheep to the slaughter, the people have put their trust in the teachings of man, from one generation to another, a never-ending story of deceit.

Throughout history mankind has **FALSELY** taken the liberty to speak on God's behalf, some for profit and power, some for vanity and self-righteousness, and some just refused to look beyond the traditions of mankind.

This type of deception has caused way too much turbulence and confusion among the people of the world, it's now time that these falsehoods are brought into the light and eradicated forever!

> "God is the BEST communicator there is, it seems irrational that one would need to speak on Gods behalf"

"The SPIRIT of TRUTH is of God, the truth cometh from God, and these words are truthful, that there is no better communicator than God...... ARE YOU LISTENING?"

"To hear the whisper of God, one must be able to distinguish the difference between the voice of their ego, and the nature of God's love"

"Listen with your heart, for everything else is just noise"

Chapter 6

THE BEGINNING OF GOD MYTHS

God myths first started with the ancients, and because they dominate our understanding of God, it's important that we understand their origin.

> "Nearly everything we know about God is based upon ancient writings"

The ancient's main source of entertainment was story-telling, and these stories became every bit as important as our televisions and cell phones are today. Some of their stories were so popular that they were told over and over again throughout the ages, and eventually they became intertwined into society.

When the written word finally became widespread, many of these stories were recorded and passed on from one generation to the next, with some of the more popular stories eventually becoming accepted as absolute truth.

We know that the early ancients believed in god(s); however, we don't know if the first ancients were directly guided by God, (as suggested in the book of Genesis) or if they just observed the nature of things around them, then using simple logic realized everything around them had a creator, and therefore they themselves did too.

We also know the ancients believed "as some still do" natural disasters were a punishment cast upon them from their god(s). So to appease their god(s) and win favor, they established many rituals and traditions, such as animal and human sacrifice. Soon ceremonial worshipping became commonplace among the people, with each tribe worshipping their own god(s), in their own way, and of course believing that their god(s) were the only true god(s).

It didn't take long for the ancients to realize they could use religion to gain power and control over the people, they also found it was much easier to rule over the people.

If anyone threatened the leaders or was disobedient, they would simply be blamed for breaking on their god(s) laws. Punishment could be harsh and deadly, and because it was all done in the name of their god(s) it was easy to justify.

These ancient cultures and traditions may seem rather barbaric, however, thousands of years later some of these traditions still exist. According to the International Humanist and Ethical Union, there are still 13 countries where atheism and blasphemy are still punishable by death.

Don't be confused, extreme Truth Blindness doesn't exist only in remote corners of the world, as cults, extremist, false doctrine, and shaming exists everywhere.

"SO STRONG ARE THE BONDS OF RELIGIOUS TRADITIONS THAT PEOPLE TODAY STILL FEAR TO QUESTION ITS AUTHENTICITY"

"God has given you a logical, reasoning mind, that you may not be led astray by the deceivers. TRUTH HAS NO FEAR"

Much like people today the early ancients were very VISUAL, their need for visual conformation first led them to worship objects such as the sun, animals, water, and fire. As the people advanced in knowledge so did their need for more realism, and eventually characters such as Buddha, Muhammad, and Jesus would fit their needs.

As the population grew, so did the difference in their beliefs. These differences ultimately lead to much dissension, and the falling-out eventually divide the people, thus creating different cultures and belief systems, many of which still exist to this day.

Because all life originated from God, including alien life, I find no reason to make alien intervention a topic of conversation. Someday we may find that alien life was responsible for helping the ancients, however, for now it's nothing more than conjecture and has little to do with the God myths we'll be discussing.

Let's summarize:

God is the best communicator there is.

The ancients knew there was a god(s); however, most were unwilling to accept an infinite God (which is still true to this day), and they instead required a visual god(s), which eventually led them to worshiping a host of many different idols, including mankind.

The ancient leaders used religion to help control the people, using harsh punishment and even death to keep them obedient.

God created all life everywhere.

Over the ages the ancients created many gods, and many stories were recorded and passed down, the most popular and most enforced stories eventually became the corner-stone of today's religions, and the GOD MYTHS that surround us in Truth Blindness.

Chapter 7

THE REVEALING OF GOD MYTHS

Many religious leaders will fear the truth this book holds, for keeping you obedient and spiritually weak is to their advantage.

Even after being shown the indisputable proof behind TRUTH BLINDNESS, many religious followers will still continue to go along with the crowd as they have for thousands of years. It has been this type of religious complacency that has led us to what we know and have today, a MAN MADE IMAGE OF GOD.

An image in which we portray and characterize God with man-made doctrines, misconceptions, deceptions, and even man's likeness. For too long now mankind has spread their vile in the name of God, saying God said this, or God said that, it's time for the truth to be revealed.

"The things of old will now be made **CLEAR**, the **REVEALING** has started, and the **TRUTH SHALL STAND FOREVER**"

Many things have been falsely communicated about God, however, the one source that has had the most influence, and has done the most damage, are the *ancient writings* that are found within the Bible, Torah, Quran, and other books of this nature.

"THE WORD OF GOD........IS TRUTH"

For thousands of years these ancient writings have been passed down from one generation to the next, they have been with us for so long that they have become imbedded into our society and into our way of thinking and learning about God.

From infants we are taught and conditioned to accept these ancient writings as the holy word of God, and one dare not question the validity. Very few have ever escaped Truth Blindness completely, and the ones that have usually taken it to the opposite extreme, becoming atheist and denouncing God altogether.

Chapter 8

SPOKEN WORD OF GOD

One of the biggest myths is the belief that all these ancient writings found in the BIBLE, TORAH, QURAN, ETC., are the actual spoken word of God.

We need only to consider the many contradictions found within these books to know that all these writings cannot be the spoken word of God, for our God is not a God of contradictions.

Even though these books do contain some truths, they also undermine God in some very deceptive and cunning ways as you'll learn later on.

I'll only be discussing in detail a few of the more pertinent contradictions, however below is a list of some of the more obvious contradictions that you may find interesting.

Contradictions may be subject to the reader's discretion, and how literal one may view them, however, there are many that are clearly irrefutable as you'll discover.

1. Genesis 2:17 Adam was to die the day he ate the forbidden fruit. "For in that day you will surely die"

    Genesis 5:5 Adam lived 930 years.

2. Genesis 4:9 God asked Cain; where is Abel your brother?

    Proverbs 15:3 The eyes of the Lord are in every place. "so why would God ask Cain"

3. Genesis 6:19-20 Noah was told to bring two of every living flesh into the ark.

    Genesis 7:2-3 You shall take seven each of every clean animal, and two each of unclean animals.

4. **Genesis 7:7** Noah entered the ark during the Flood.

   Genesis 7:12-13 The rain was on the earth 40 days and 40 nights, on the very same day Noah entered the ark.

5. **Genesis 11:29** Abraham married his half-sister and was blessed.

   Deuteronomy 27:22 Cursed is the one who lies with his sister, the daughter of his father or the daughter of his mother.

6. **2 Samuel 24:1** The Lord moved David to go number Israel and Judah.

   1 Chronicles 21:1 Satan moved David to number Israel.

7. **2 Kings 24:8** Jehoiachin was 18 years old when he became king.

   2 Chronicles 36:9 Jehoiachin was 8 years old when he became king.

8. **Genesis 32:28-30** Jacob is renamed Israel at Peniel.

Genesis 35:10-15 Jacob is renamed in Bethel.

9. **Genesis 26:32-33 Isaac's servants dug a well at Beer-shebah**

   Genesis 21:30-31 Abraham dug a well at Beer- shebah

10. **Genesis 26:34 Esau took as his wives Judith and Basemath.**

    Genesis 36:2-3 Esau took for his wives Adah, Aholibamah, and Basemath.

11. **Exodus 18:17-24 Moses father-in-law came up with the idea to have judges for the people.**

    Deuteronomy 1:9-18 Moses never mentions judges were his father-in-law's idea.

12. **2 Samuel 24:9 There were 500,000 fighting men in Judah.**

    1 Chronicles 21:5 There were 470,000 fighting men.

13. **Exodus 3:1 Moses father-in-law's name was Jethro.**

Numbers 10:29 Moses father-in-law's name was Reuel.

14. **Exodus 24:2 Moses alone shall come near the Lord**

    Exodus 24:9-11 Moses, Aaron, Nadab, Abihu, and seventy of the elders all saw God.

15. **Numbers 21:6 The Lord sent fiery serpents among the people, they bit the people and many died.**

    The Ten Commandments says thou shall not kill

16. **Jeremiah 7:22 The Lord says I did not speak to your fathers, or command them concerning burnt offerings or sacrifices.**

    Exodus 20:24 An alter of earth you shall make for me, and you shall sacrifice on it your burnt offerings, your sheep and oxen.

17. **Numbers 20:27 Aaron died on Mount Hor.**

Deuteronomy 10:6 Aaron died at Moserah.

18. 2 Samuel 8:4 David captured 700 horsemen.

    1 Chronicles David captured 7000 horsemen.

19. Numbers 33:41-42 After Aaron died, the people moved from Mount Hor to Zalmonah to Punon.

    Deuteronomy 10:6-7 After Aaron dies, the people moved from Moserah to Gudgodah to Jotbathah.

20. Numbers 21:3 And the Canaanites were utterly destroyed.

    Judges 3:3-4 The Canaanites were left that the Lord might test Israel, to know if they would obey the commandments of the Lord.

21. 1 Samuel 15:20 Saul utterly destroyed the Amalekites.

    1 Samuel 27:8-9 David raided the Amalekites and they left neither man nor woman alive.

22. Samuel 28:6 Saul inquired of the Lord, but the Lord did not answer him.

    1 Chronicles 10:14 Saul did not inquire of the Lord, therefore he killed him.

23. 1 Chronicles 10:4 Therefore Saul took a sword and fell on it.

    2 Samuel 21:12 The Philistines struck down Saul in Gilboa.

    1 Chronicles 10:14 Saul didn't inquire of the Lord, therefore the Lord killed him.

24. 1 Samuel 16:10-11 Jesse has eight sons.

    1 Chronicles 2:13-15 Jesse has seven sons.

25. Joshua 10:38-39 Joshua utterly destroyed Debir.

    Judges 1:11-13 Othniel took Debir.

26. 2 Samuel 24:9 Israel had 800,000 men that drew the sword, and Judah had 500,000.

1 Chronicles 21:5 Israel had 1,100,000 men that drew the sword, Judah had 470,000.

27. **1 Kings 9:28** They brought back 420 talents of gold from Ophir.

    2 Chronicles 8:18 They brought back 450 talents of gold from Ophir.

28. **1 Samuel 16:19** Saul sent messengers to Jesse, David's father, asking him to send his son David.

    1 Samuel 17:58 And Saul said to David, whose son are you.

29. **2 Samuel 6:23** Michal had no children.

    2 Samuel 21:8 Michal had five sons.

30. **1 Kings 15:5** David's only once turned from Lord in the matter of Uriah the Hittite.

    1 Samuel 24:9-10 David sinned by numbering the people.

31. **2 Samuel 24:24** David paid 50 shekels of silver for the property.

1 Chronicles 21:25 David paid 600 pieces of gold for the property.

32. 1 Kings 4:26 Solomon had 40,000 stalls of horses.

2 Chronicles 9:25 Solomon had 4,000 stalls of horses.

33. 1 Kings 5:16 Solomon had 3300 men to supervise.

2 Chronicles 2:2 Solomon had 3600 men to supervise.

34. 1 Kings 7:26 There were 2000 baths

2 Chronicles 4:5 There were 3000 baths

35. 2 Kings 18:1-5 There was no greater king before or after Hezekiah.

2 Kings 23:24-25 There was no greater king before or after Josiah.

36. 2 Kings 8:26 Ahaziah was twenty-two years old when he began to rule.

2 Chronicles 22:2 Ahaziah was forty-two when he began to rule.

37. Exodus 23:7 God says one should not kill the innocent.

    Numbers 31:17 God commands them to kill the young males and women.

38. Numbers 11:33 God caused sickness.

    Job 2:7 Satan caused sickness.

39. Exodus 34:7 God doesn't forget sins.

    Jeremiah 31:34 God says I will forgive their iniquity, and their sin I will remember no more.

40. Judges 4:21 Sisera was sleeping when Jael killed him.

    Judges 5:25-27 Sisera fell to the floor after being struck and killed by Jael.

41. 2 Chronicles 2-3 Asa removed the high places.

    1 Kings 15:14 Asa did not remove the high places.

42. 1 Kings 16:6-8 Baasha died in the 26th year of king Asa.

2 Chronicles 16:1 Baasha built the city of Ramah in the 36th year of king Asa.

43. 2 Samuel 24:13 David had the option of seven years of famine.

   1 Chronicles 21:12 David had the option of three years of famine.

44. Ezra 2:65 There were 200 singers.

   Nehemiah 7:67 There were 245 singers

45. Matthew 14:5 Herod wanted to kill John the Baptist.

   Mark 6:19-20 Herod tried to protect John the Baptist.

46. Matthew 9:9 Jesus saw Matthew in the tax office and said follow me.

   Mark 2:14 Jesus saw Levi in the tax office and said follow me.

47. Mark 14:32-42 Jesus went off and prayed three different times.

Luke 22:39-46 Jesus only went off to pray once.

48. **Mark 15:39** The centurion said when Jesus died, truly this was the son of God.

    Luke 23:47 The centurion said when Jesus died, certainly this man was a righteous man.

49. **Mark 15:34** Jesus said My God, my God, why have you forsaken me, speaking in Aramaic.

    Matthew 27:46 Jesus spoke those last words in Hebrew.

50. God limited the life span of humans to 120 years (Genesis 6:3)

    Since then many people have lived much longer than 120 years.

51. **John 3:13** No one but Jesus has ascended to heaven.

    2 Kings 2:11 Elijah ascended into heaven in a whirlwind.

52. **Mark 16:1** After the Sabbath they bought spices.

    Luke 23:55 – 24:1 They prepared the spices the day before the Sabbath.

53. **Matthew 28:9** Mary Magdalene and the other Mary met Jesus on their way back from his tomb, they held him by his feet and worshiped him.

    John 20:1-17 Mary is alone when she meets Jesus, Jesus tells her not to cling to him.

54. **Exodus 7:20-21** Moses turned all the water into blood.

    Exodus 7:22 The pharaohs magicians then did the same. "How was it possible for the magicians to turn the water into blood if Moses already did"

55. **1 Corinthians 15:5** After his resurrection Jesus appeared to 11 of his disciples.

    Mark 16:14 Jesus appeared to 12 disciples.

Chapter 9

INSPIRED WORD OF GOD

Because knowledge has increased so much over the last few years, more people have come to accept these ancient writings as the INSPIRED WORD OF GOD, in place of the ACTUAL SPOKEN WORD OF GOD. So let's take a moment to look at these writings from that perspective.

Because of the many contradictions found within these books, we can only conclude most of these writings were based upon myths that were passed down, and stories that sole purpose was to benefit the leaders. If any of these writings were purposely inspired by God, only God could answer that.

One must never throw their objectivity out the window, for God would not have you be deceived, therefore, one must constantly be observing and asking questions when discerning the truth. When we read these ancient books, we must keep this in mind.

One may say that these ancient writings were inspired by God, but it doesn't necessarily make it so. One's own inspiration may be nothing more than EGO, or a terrible interpretation of the truth. The following are excellent examples of inspiration gone astray.

At the Jonestown Massacre 918 men, women, and children died in vain, their inspiration being misguided and reckless.

The Order of the Soar Temple where 74 members committed suicide, believing they were moving on to Sirius, this tragedy was falsely inspired.

There was 39 Heaven's Gate follower's that committed suicide, believing that their souls could journey aboard a spaceship that was following the comet Hale-Bopp, once again more **FALSE INSPIRATION.**

The Branch Davidians in Waco, Texas 87 people died, more **FALSE INSPIRATION.**

19 hijackers believing they were doing God's will on 9/11, took the lives of 2977 innocent people. They were so **HIGHLY INSPIRED** they were willing to **SACRIFICE THEIR OWN LIVES.**

For all of the above, their inspiration, their very faith, was nothing more than misplaced trust. In each group there was a leader these people trusted with their very souls, Jim Jones, David Koresh, Marshall Applewhite, Osama bin Laden, Joseph Di Mambro and Luc Jouret, all of them religious leaders that in some way truly believed they were doing God's work, but in reality they were listening to their own **EGO !!**

People that do evil as the ones mentioned above are a perfect example of a controlling **EGO.** They start believing themselves to be specially ordained by God, believing their own thoughts are those of God. At this stage we find that it's not long before their downfall usually begins.

"ANY RELIGION OR FAITH THAT CONDONES MURDER AND SUICIDE IS NOT OF GOD"

Let's summarize: The spirit of TRUTH, is of God.

We truthfully don't know if God spoke or inspired any of these ancient writings, for only God could answer that.

Conjecture is not truth.

Never be afraid to test what is truth.

Chapter 10

CREATION MYTHS REVEALED

Nearly every culture that has ever existed has a creation story, as there is no shortage of them. Research shows there is well over 100 known creation myths, many that can easily be found online.

Currently though, the creation story in the book of Genesis, and the Big Bang theory, are the two most popular explanations for the **CREATION** of humankind.

Although **NEITHER CAN BE PROVED AND THEY'RE BOTH BASED ON ASSUMPTIONS**, because they are widely viewed as factual we'll take some time to discuss them.

Chapter 11

GENESIS CREATION

For, **THOUSANDS OF YEARS** the creation story in Genesis has been **ENFORCED** and **IMBEDDED** in the mind of most believers. In some countries **ENFORCEMENT** could mean a death sentence for a non-believer, while in other countries like the United States it usually involves the shaming and ridicule of non-believers, such as being told they're going to hell, they're a sinner, or they won't be saved.

For most believers and non-believers these religious **ENFORCEMENTS** usually start during early childhood when the mind is young and more easily conditioned to accept myth as truth. As one ages these myths can become so deeply entrenched in the mind, that any chance of breaking free becomes nearly impossible.

After being enforced for thousands of years through religious traditions and persecution, these myths prove to be brainwashing at its best. The effects can be **DEVASTATING** for the believer, as they freely relinquish their objectivity to mankind's doctrine.

GENESIS CREATION FACTS

When we look at the book of Genesis there are two things we must consider, who wrote it, and is it truth worthy.

Traditionally Moses is credited with writing Genesis, however; there is no definitive proof that someone named Moses, as portrayed in the ancient writings ever existed.

There's also no definitive proof that there was ever an Exodus out of Egypt led by Moses.

Another problem with the Exodus story is that the name of the Egyptian pharaoh was conveniently never mention.

There appears to be several different writing styles which indicate multiple authors.

The creation story Moses supposedly wrote about "word for word" happened around 2500 years before his birth.

It's highly unlikely that God almighty needed to rest on the seventh day. Isaiah 40:28 Hast thou not known? Hast thou not heard, *that* the everlasting God, the LORD, the Creator of the ends of the earth, fainteth not, neither is weary?

> "Although Sunday is treated as the Sabbath day for most, if you look at a calendar Saturday is actually the last day of the week"

For one to believe the Genesis story is true, then one must also believe there was a talking serpent.

Even though the location is described in Genesis, the Garden of Eden has never been located.

Similar stories about The Tree of Life and the Tree of Knowledge can be found in other cultures. "Consider the Adam and

Eve cylinder seal, located at the British Museum, a very interesting artifact"

GOD IS ALL KNOWING: However, according to Genesis 3:9-11 God asked Adam who told him he was naked, and if he had eaten from the tree. Also in Genesis 4:9-10 God asked Cain where Abel was and what had he done. Because God is all knowing, these questions don't seem probable.

According to the book of Jubilees, it claims Cain married his sister Awan. It also mentions that Seth (the third son of Adam and Eve) married his sister Azura. "However, incest is forbidden"

In Genesis 6:19 it's written God told Noah to bring TWO of every sort into the ark, male and female......Then in Genesis 7:2 it's written God told Noah you shall take with you SEVEN each of every clean animal, male and female; two each of unclean animals; also SEVEN each of birds of the air.

The story of Noah and the great flood is the regeneration of earth, thus it's the second Genesis.

Similar to creation stories, flood stories are also common among nearly every culture, with many of these stories similar to the Noah myth.

If Googled, one can see there is no shortage of creation or flood stories.

When we review the Genesis story objectively, when we consider the real facts, there is no actual proof that the story is anything more than ancient myth.

"One must never lose their objectivity to question what is and isn't TRUTH, and therefore what is and isn't of GOD"

Chapter 12

THE BIG BANG MYTH

The next most widely recognized creation story is called the Big Bang Theory. Taught in nearly every science class, the Big Bang Theory is the atheist community's most popular explanation on how the universe came into existence.

The **BIG BANG THEORY** is usually thought of as a single point of very high-density and temperature, sometimes referred to as the singularity. It's the inflation of the singularity "**BIG BANG**" that is supposedly responsible for creating and expanding our universe.

"Astronomer Fred Hoyle is credited with the term "big bang", Hoyle however, described the theory as IRRATIONAL."

*"Our universe is thought to have begun as an infinitesimally small, infinitely hot, infinitely dense, something - a singularity. {Singularities are zones which defy our current understanding of physics} Where did it come from? We don't know. Why did it appear? We don't know."**

*big-bang-theory.com

When we research the BIG BANG THEORY, it doesn't take long to see it's plagued with problems upon problems, some being so chaotic they require theories for the theory.

For more information simply Google: "problems associated with the Big Bang theory"

Below is an article by Plasma physicist and author Eric Lerner, it's a letter that has been published, and endorsed by many.

I searched out Eric for permission to use his article as I firmly believe he gives an accurate and truthful account of the Big Bang theory. Thanks Eric.

An Open Letter to the Scientific Community
cosmologystatement.org

The big bang today relies on a growing number of hypothetical entities, things that we have never observed-- inflation, dark matter and dark energy are the most prominent examples. Without them, there would be a fatal contradiction between the observations made by astronomers and the predictions of the big bang theory. In no other field of physics would this continual recourse to new hypothetical objects be accepted as a way of bridging the gap between theory and observation. It would, at the least, raise serious questions about the validity of the underlying theory.

But the big bang theory can't survive without these fudge factors. Without the hypothetical inflation field, the big bang does not predict the smooth, isotropic cosmic background radiation that is observed, because there would be no way for parts of the universe that are now more than a few degrees away in the sky to come to the same temperature and thus emit the same amount of microwave radiation.

Without some kind of dark matter, unlike any that we have observed on Earth despite 20 years of experiments, big-bang theory makes contradictory predictions for the density of matter in the universe. Inflation requires a density 20 times larger than that implied by big bang nucleosynthesis, the theory's explanation of the origin of the light elements. And without dark energy, the theory predicts that the universe is only about 8 billion years old, which is billions of years younger than the age of many stars in our galaxy.

What is more, the big bang theory can boast of no quantitative predictions that have subsequently been validated by observation. The successes claimed by the theory's supporters consist of its ability to retrospectively fit observations with a steadily increasing array of adjustable parameters, just as the old Earth-centered cosmology of Ptolemy needed layer upon layer of epicycles.

Yet the big bang is not the only framework available for understanding the history of the universe. Plasma cosmology and the steady-state model both hypothesize an evolving universe without beginning or end. These and other alternative approaches can also explain the basic phenomena of the cosmos, including the abundances of light elements, the generation of large-scale structure, the cosmic background radiation, and how the redshift of far-away galaxies increases with distance. They have even predicted new phenomena that were subsequently observed, something the big bang has failed to do.

Supporters of the big bang theory may retort that these theories do not explain every cosmological observation. But that is scarcely surprising, as their development has been severely hampered by a complete lack of funding. Indeed, such questions and alternatives cannot even now be freely discussed and examined. An open exchange of ideas is lacking in most mainstream conferences. Whereas

Richard Feynman could say that "science is the culture of doubt", in cosmology today doubt and dissent are not tolerated, and young scientists learn to remain silent if they have something negative to say about the standard big bang model. Those who doubt the big bang fear that saying so will cost them their funding.

Even observations are now interpreted through this biased filter, judged right or wrong depending on whether or not they support the big bang. So discordant data on red shifts, lithium and helium abundances, and galaxy distribution, among other topics, are ignored or ridiculed. This reflects a growing dogmatic mindset that is alien to the spirit of free scientific inquiry.

Today, virtually all financial and experimental resources in cosmology are devoted to big bang studies. Funding comes from only a few sources, and all the peer-review committees that control them are dominated by supporters of the big bang. As a result, the dominance of the big bang within the field has become self-sustaining, irrespective of the scientific validity of the theory.

Giving support only to projects within the big bang framework undermines a fundamental element of the scientific method -- the constant testing of theory against observation. Such a restriction makes unbiased discussion and research impossible. To redress this, we urge those agencies that fund work in cosmology to set aside a significant fraction of their funding for investigations into alternative theories and observational contradictions of the big bang. To avoid bias, the peer review committee that allocates such funds could be composed of astronomers and physicists from outside the field of cosmology.

Allocating funding to investigations into the big bang's validity, and its alternatives, would allow the scientific process to determine our most accurate model of the history of the universe.

Signed:
(Institutions for identification only)

Halton Arp, Max-Planck-Institute Für Astrophysik (Germany)

Andre Koch Torres Assis, State University of Campinas (Brazil)

Yuri Baryshev, Astronomical Institute, St. Petersburg State University (Russia)

Ari Brynjolfsson, Applied Radiation Industries (USA)

Hermann Bondi, Churchill College, University of Cambridge (UK)

Timothy Eastman, Plasmas International (USA)

Chuck Gallo, Superconix, Inc.(USA)

Thomas Gold, Cornell University (emeritus) (USA)

Amitabha Ghosh, Indian Institute of Technology, Kanpur (India)

Walter J. Heikkila, University of Texas at Dallas (USA)

Michael Ibison, Institute for Advanced Studies at Austin (USA)

Thomas Jarboe, University of Washington (USA)
Jerry W. Jensen, ATK Propulsion (USA)
Menas Kafatos, George Mason University (USA)
Eric J. Lerner, Lawrenceville Plasma Physics (USA)
Paul Marmet, Herzberg Institute of Astrophysics (Canada)
Paola Marziani, Istituto Nazionale di Astrofisica, Osservatorio Astronomico di Padova (Italy)
Gregory Meholic, The Aerospace Corporation (USA)
Jacques Moret-Bailly, Université Dijon (retired) (France)
Jayant Narlikar, IUCAA(emeritus) and College de France (India, France)
Marcos Cesar Danhoni Neves, State University of Maringá (Brazil)
Charles D. Orth, Lawrence Livermore National Laboratory (USA)
R. David Pace, Lyon College (USA)
Georges Paturel, Observatoire de Lyon (France)
Jean-Claude Pecker, College de France (France)
Anthony L. Peratt, Los Alamos National Laboratory (USA)
Bill Peter, BAE Systems Advanced Technologies (USA)
David Roscoe, Sheffield University (UK)
Malabika Roy, George Mason University (USA)
Sisir Roy, George Mason University (USA)
Konrad Rudnicki, Jagiellonian University (Poland)
Domingos S.L. Soares, Federal University of Minas Gerais (Brazil)
John L. West, Jet Propulsion Laboratory, California Institute of Technology (USA)

James F. Woodward, California State University, Fullerton (USA)
Jorge Marao, Universidade Estadual de Londrina, Brazil
Martin John Baker, Loretto School Musselburgh, UK
Peter J. Carroll, Psychonaut Institute, UK
Roger Y. Gouin, Ecole Supérieure d'Electricité, France
John Murray, Sunyata Composite Ltd, UK
Jonathan Chambers, University of Sheffield, UK
Michel A. Duguay, Laval University, Canada
Qi Pan, Fitzwilliam College, Cambridge, UK
Fred Rost, University of NSW (Emeritus), Australia
Louis Hissink, Consulting Geologist, Australia
Hetu Sheth, Earth Sciences, Indian Institute of Technology Bombay, India
Lassi Hyvärinen, IBM (Retired), France
Max Whisson, University of Melbourne, Australia
R. S. Griffiths, CADAS, UK
Adolf Muenker, Brane Industries, USA
Emre Isik, Akdeniz University, Turkey
Felipe de Oliveira Alves, Federal University of Minas Gerais, Brazil
Jean-Marc Bonnet-Bidaud, Service d'Astrophysique, CEA, France
Kim George, Curtin University of Technology, Australia
Tom Van Flandern, Meta Research, USA
Doneley Watson, IBM (Retired), USA
Fred Alan Wolf, Have Brains/Will Travel, USA
Robert Wood, IEEE, Canada
D. W. Harris, L-3 Communications, USA

Eugene Sittampalam, Engineering consultant, Sri Lanka
Joseph. B. Krieger, Brooklyn College, CUNY, USA
Pablo Vasquez, New Jersey Institute of Technology, USA
Peter F. Richiuso, NASA, KSC, USA
Roger A. Rydin, University of Virginia (Emeritus), USA
Stefan Rydstrom, Royal Institute of Technology, Sweden
Sylvan J. Hotch, The MITRE Corporation (Retired), USA
Thomas R. Love, CSU Dominguez Hills, USA
Andrew Coles, Embedded Systems, USA
Eit Gaastra, Infinite universe researcher, The Netherlands
Franco Selleri, Università di Bari, Dipartimento di Fisica, Italy
Gerald Pease, The Aerospace Corporation, USA
S.N. Arteha, Space Research Institute, Russia
Miroslaw Kozlowski, Warsaw University (Emeritus), Poland
John Hartnett, School of Physics, University of Western Australia, Australia
Robert Zubrin, Pioneer Astronautics, USA
Tibor Gasparik, SUNY at Stony Brook, USA
Alexandre Losev, Bulgarian Academy of Sciences, Bulgaria
Henry Hall, University of Manchester, UK
José da Silva, Universidade Federal de Minas Gerais, Brazil
Markus Rohner, Griesser AG, Switzerland

William C. Mitchell, Institute for Advanced Cosmological Studies, USA
Aurea Garcia-Rissmann, UFSC, Brazil
Cristian R. Ghezzi, Universidade Estadual de Campinas, Brazil
Daniel Nicolato Epitácio Pereira, Federal University of Rio de Janeiro, Brazil
Gregory M. Salyards, US Naval Sea Systems Command (Retired), USA
Luiz Carlos Barbosa, Unicamp, Brazil
Luiz Carlos Jafelice, Federal University of the Rio Grande do Norte, Brazil
Michael Sosteric, Athabasca University, Canada
Steven Langley Guy, University of Elizabeth (Physics Department), Australia
Robert Fritzius, Shade Tree Physics, USA
Irineu Gomes Varella, Escola Municipal de Astrofísica, Brazil
Tom Walther, Southern Cross University Australia, Australia
Mauro Cosentino, University of São Paulo, Brazil
Moacir Lacerda, Univeersidade Federal de Mato Grosso do Sul, Brazil
Roberto Assumpcao, PUC Minas, Brazil
Roberto Lopes Parra, University of Sao Paulo, Brazil
Ronaldo Junio Camppos Batista, Universidade Federal de Minas Gerais, Brazil
Ermenegildo Caccese, University of Basilicata, Italy
Felipe Sofia Zanuzzo, Federal University of São Carlos, Brazil
Edival de Morais, Sociedade Brasileira de Física, Brazil

Graham Coupe, KAZ Technology Services, Australia
Gordon Petrie, High Altitude Observatory, NCAR, USA
Jose B. Almeida, University of Minho, Portugal
Antonio Cleiton, Laboratório de Sistemas Complexos - UFPI, Brazil
Sergey Karpov, L.V. Kirensky Institute of Physics Russian Academy of Sciences, Russia
Wagner Patrick Junqueira de Souza Coelho Nicácio, Universidade Federal de Minas Gerais, Brazil
Sokolov Vladimir, Special Astrophysical Observatory of RAS, Russia
Edwin G. Schasteen, TAP-TEN Research Foundation International, USA
Gerry Zeitlin, openseti.org, USA
Henry H. Bauer, Virginia Polytechnic Institute & State University, USA
Yasha Fard, H.R. Cosmology Institute, Canada
Roberto Caimmi, Astronomy Department, Padua University, Italy
Tobias Keller, ETH (SFIT) Zurich, Earth Sciences, Switzerland
Deborah Foch, Center for the Study of Extraterrestrial Intelligence, USA
Henry Reynolds, UC Santa Cruz, USA
Paramahamsa Tewari, Nuclear Power Corporation (Retired), India
Jouko Seppänen, Helsinki University of Technology, Finland
Cristiane Ribeiro Bernardes, Universidade Federal de Minas Gerais, Brazil
Eric Blievernicht, TRW, USA

Dr. Robert Bennett, Kolbe Center, USA
Hilton Ratcliffe, Astronomical Society of South Africa, South Africa
Wieslaw Sztumski, Silesian University, Poland
Lars Wåhlin, Colutron Research Corporation, USA
Riccardo Scarpa, European Southern Observatory, Italy
Olivier Marco, European Southern Observatory, France
Joseph Garcia, International Radiation Protection, Germany
Arkadiusz Jadczyk, International Institute of Mathematical Physics, Lithuania
Jean de Pontcharra, Commissariat à l'Energie Atomique, France
Gerardus D. Bouw, Baldwin-Wallace College, USA
Josef Lutz, Chemnitz University of Technology, Germany
Harold E. Puthoff, Institute for Advanced Studies at Austin, USA
Hermann Dürkop, Nabla Systemberatung, Germany
Klaus Fischer, Universität Trier, Germany
Werner Holzmüller, University Leipzig, Germany
Sol Aisenberg, International Technology Group, USA
Richard Gancarczyk, University of Nottingham, UK
Steve Humphry, Murdoch University, Australia
Alberto Bolognesi, Università di Perugia, Italy
Daniele Carosati, Armenzano Observatory, Italy
Brendan Dean, H.R. Cosmology Institute, Canada
W. Jim Jastrzebski, Warsaw University, Poland
Gero Rupprecht, European Southern Observatory, Germany

Rainer Herrmann, TEWS-Elektronik, Germany
Felix Pharand, University of Montreal, Canada
Jerry Bergman, Northwest State University, USA
Sinan Alis, Eyuboglu Twin Observatories, Turkey
Esat Rennan, Pekünlü University of EGE, Turkey
Anne M. Hofmeister, Washington U., USA
Quentin Foreman, IEEE, New Zealand
Marc Berndl, University of Toronto, Canada
Y. P. Varshni, University of Ottawa, Canada
Robert Martinek, McMaster University, Canada
Bob Criss, Washington University, USA
Paul LaViolette, The Starburst Foundation, USA
Seetesh Pandé, Université Claude Bernard, Lyon France
Tahir Maqsood, PSA, Pakistan
Hartmut Traunmüller, University of Stockholm, Sweden
Nico F. Benschop, Amspade Research, The Netherlands
Aaron Blake, USAF, USA
M. Ross Fergus, University of Memphis, USA
Sonu Bhaskar, Council of Scientific and Industrial Research, India
V. F. Frederico, Lima Universidade de Sao Paulo, Brazil
Andrei Kirilyuk, Institute of Metal Physics of the National Academy of Sciences of Ukraine, Ukraine
Christian Jooss, Institut für Materialphysik, University of Goettingen, Germany
Robert O. Myers, ROM Technologies, USA
Ana Cristina Oliveira, Universidade Federal de Minas Gerais, Brazil
John Wey, Idaho National Laboratory, USA

Jorge Francisco Maldonado Serrano, UIS, Colombia
Pasquale Galianni, Dipartimento di Fisica Università di Lecce, Italy
Martín López-Corredoira, Instituto de Astrofísica de Canarias, Spain
Michael A. Ivanov, Belarus State University of Informatics and Radioelectronics, Belarus
Xiao Jianhua , Shanghai Jiaotong University, China
Pierre J. Beaujon, Hoornbeeck College, The Netherlands
J. Georg von Brzeski, Helios Labs, USA
Vidyardhi Nanduri, Cosmology Research center, India
Mike Rotch, NBSA, USA
Paul Noel, independent researcher, USA
Swee Eng, AW Royal College of Pathologists, Singapore
Ricardo Rodríguez, La Laguna University, Spain
Linda Camp, Harvard University, USA
James B. Schwartz, The Noah's Ark Research Foundation, Philippines
Marshall Douglas Smith, TeddySpeaks Foundation, USA
Abbé Grumel, Association Copernic, France
Ives van Leth, Waterboard Utrecht, The Netherlands
Francis Michael C. Perez, Department of Transportation, USA
Ahmed A. El-Dash, Unicamp, Brazil
David C Ware, University of Auckland, New Zealand
Alek Atevik, Skopje Astronomy Society, Macedonia
Peter Rowlands, University of Liverpool, UK
Robert Day, Suntola Consulting, Ltd., USA

Luís Paulo Sousa Loureiro, Portugal
Maingot Fabrice, Université Louis Pasteur, France
Kris Krogh, University of California, USA
Pierre-Marie Robitaille, The Ohio State University, USA
Charles Creager Jr, Creation Research Society, USA
Stephan Gift, The University of the West Indies, St Augustine Campus, Trinidad and Tobago
Joseph J. Smulsky, Institute of Earth's Cryosphere Siberian Branch Russian Academy of Sciences, Russia
Jim O'Reilly, Orion Consultants, USA
Robert MacKay, University of Warwick, UK
Chris Vermeulen, Astronomical Society of Southern Africa, South Africa
Emilson Pereira, Leite Institute of Astronomy and Geophysics, Brazil
Allen W. Green, ATK Space Systems, USA
Ron Balsys, Central Queensland University, Australia
Paul ten Boom, University of New South Wales, Australia
Mosheh Thezion, The Empirical Church, USA
Karsten Markus, Wilhelm-Foerster-Observatory Berlin e.V, Germany
Don C. Wilson, Process Technology and Development, USA
Marek Gajewski, Raytheon Co., USA
Tuncay Dogan, University of EGE, Turkey
Andrew M. Uhl, Pennsylvania State Univeristy, USA
Klaus Wieder, independent researcher, Germany
John Caley, Omegafour Pty Ltd, Australia

Keith Scott-Mumby, Capital University for Integrative Medicine/California, Institute for Human Sciences, USA
Garth A Barber, independent researcher, UK
Dean L. Mamas, independent researcher, USA
David Blackford, independent researcher, UK
Alan Rees, independent researcher, Sweden
Udayan Chakravarty, independent researcher, India
Georg Gane, independent researcher, Germany
Robin Whittle, independent researcher, Australia
Joseph A. Rybczyk, independent researcher, USA
G.Srinivasan, independent researcher, India
Geoffrey E. Willcher, independent researcher, USA
Douglas S. Robbemond, independent researcher, The Netherlands
Khosrow Fariborzi, independent researcher, Iran
Etienne Bielen, independent researcher, Belgium
Steve Newman, independent researcher, USA
Ethan Skyler, independent researcher, USA
Yvon Dufour, independent researcher, Canada
Jorge Ales Corona, independent researcher, Spain
Cristiano De Angelis, independent researcher, Italy
Roland Le Houillier, independent researcher, Canada
Richard Tobey, independent researcher, USA
Steve McMahon, independent researcher, USA
Eugene Savov, independent researcher, Bulgaria
Lars Woldseth, independent researcher, Norway
Robert L. Brueck, independent researcher, USA
Mark S Thornhill, independent researcher, UK
Nainan. K. Varghese, independent researcher, India

Andrew Kulikovsky, independent researcher, Australia
Charles Sven, independent researcher, USA
Gabriele Manzotti, independent researcher, Italy
Brian S. Clark, independent researcher, USA
Thomas G. Franzel, independent researcher, USA
Bernhard Reddemann, independent researcher, Germany
Ives van Leth Waterboard, Utrecht, The Netherlands
Jeroen van der Rijst, independent researcher, The Netherlands
Harry Costas, independent researcher, Australia
Andrei Wasylyk, independent researcher, Canada
Jack Ruijs, independent researcher, The Netherlands
Leo Sarasúa, independent researcher, The Netherlands
Edward Smith, independent researcher, USA
Gary Meade, independent researcher, USA
Stan Kabacinski, independent researcher, Australia
Jack Dejong, independent researcher, USA
Nigel Edwards, independent researcher, Australia
Dieter Schumacher, independent researcher, Germany
Rudolf Kiesslinger, independent researcher, Germany
Gerd Schulte, independent researcher, Germany
Stuart Eves, independent researcher, UK
James Marsen, independent researcher, USA
Edgar Paternina, independent researcher, Colombia
Donald E. Scott, independent researcher, USA
José M. Cat Casanovas, independent researcher, Spain
Aaron Hill, independent researcher, USA

Hans-Dieter Radecke, independent researcher, Germany
Mawell P Davis, independent researcher, New Zealand
Gordon E. Mackay, independent researcher, USA
Dave Sagar, independent researcher, USA
Benjamin I. Iglesias, independent researcher, Spain
Alper Kozan, independent researcher, Turkey
Hartmut Warm, independent researcher, Germany
Jan Mugele, independent researcher, Germany
Andrew Rigg, independent researcher, Australia
Thomas Riedel, independent researcher, Denmark
Helen Workman, independent researcher, Canada
Morris Anderson, independent researcher, USA
Mario Cosentino, independent researcher, France
Paul Richard Price, independent researcher, USA
Philip Lilien, independent researcher, USA
Ott Köstner, independent researcher, Estonia
Bozidar Kornic, independent researcher, USA
William F. Hamilton, independent researcher, USA
Joel Morrison, independent researcher, USA
James R. Frass, independent researcher, Canada
Arnold Wittkamp, independent researcher, The Netherlands
Dimi Chakalov, independent researcher, Bulgaria
Herb Doughty, independent researcher, USA
Robert F. Beck, independent researcher, UK
Tuomo Suntola, independent researcher, Finland
Richard Hillgrove, independent researcher, New Zealand
Herbert J. Spencer, independent researcher, Canada
Thomas B. Andrews, independent researcher, USA

John Dean, independent researcher, South Africa
Peter Loster, independent researcher, Germany
Charles Francis, independent researcher, UK
Ahmed Mowaffaq AlAnni, independent researcher, Iraq
Mogens Wegener, independent researcher, Denmark
Peter Jakubowski, independent researcher, Germany
John Brodix Merryman Jr., independent researcher, USA
Christian Boland, independent researcher, Belgium
Warren S. Taylor, independent researcher, USA
Constantin Leshan, independent researcher, Moldova
Avid Samwaru, independent researcher, USA
Thomas Goodey, independent researcher, UK
Johan Masreliez, independent researcher, USA
Efrèn Cañedo, independent researcher, Mèxico
Michael Bliznetsov, independent researcher, Russia
Peter Michalicka, independent researcher, Austria
Ivan D. Alexander, independent researcher, USA
S. Ray DeRusse, independent researcher, USA
Chris Maharaj, independent researcher, Trinidad
Peter Warlow, independent researcher, UK
Gordon Wheeler, independent researcher, USA
Boxer Ma, independent researcher, Thailand
Robert Wido, independent researcher, USA
John Hunter, independent researcher, UK
Marcelo de Almeida Bueno, independent researcher, Brazil
Jean-Pierre Ady Fenyo, independent researcher, USA
Adam W.L. Chan, independent researcher, Hong Kong

Renato Giussani, independent researcher, Italy
Mustafa Kemal Oyman, independent researcher, Turkey
Richard Wayte, independent researcher, UK
Ron Ragusa, independent researcher USA
N.Vivian Pope, independent researcher, UK
Roy Caswell, independent researcher, UK
Erin S. Myers, independent researcher, USA
Ugo Nwaozuzu, independent researcher, Singapore
Daniel Coman, independent researcher, USA
Birgid Mueller, independent researcher, Mexico
Mihail Gonta, independent researcher, Moldova
Vladimir Rogozhin, independent researcher, Russia
J. J. Weissmuller, independent researcher, USA
Muhammed Anwar, independent researcher, India
Geldtmeijer Djamidin, independent researcher, The Netherlands
Scott G. Beach, independent researcher, Canada
Neil Hargreaves, independent researcher, UK
Julian Braggins, independent researcher, Australia
Kari Saarikoski, independent researcher, Finland
Ghertza Roman, independent researcher, Romania
Roland Schubert, independent researcher, Germany
Alexandre Wajnberg, independent researcher, Skyne, Belgium
Dennis H. Cowdrick, scientific independent researcher, USA
Michail Telegin, independent researcher, Russia
Robert L. Stafford, independent researcher, USA
Martin Sach, independent researcher, UK
Charles L. Sanders, independent researcher, USA/ South Korea

Alex Carlson, independent researcher, USA
Lyndon Ashmore, independent researcher, UK
Liedmann, Matthias, unaffiliated scientific researcher, Germany
Ingvar Astrand, independent researcher, Sweden
Olli Santavuori, independent researcher, Finland
JR Croca, independent researcher, Portugal
Gerard Zonus, independent researcher, France
David W. Knight, independent researcher, USA
Marcel Lutttgens, independent researcher, France
Dr Stephen Birch, independent researcher, UK
Abramyan G.L., independent researcher, Russia
Martin Peprnik, independent researcher, Slowakia
Van Den Hauwe, PhD, independent researcher, Belgium
Daniel Toohey, independent researcher, Australia
Jed Shlackman, M.S. Ed. (LMHC, C.Ht.), independent researcher, USA
Dr. John Michael Nahay, independent researcher
Guido Grzinic, independent researcher, Australia
Charles Weber, USA
David Gershon, USA
Peter G. Smith, USA
Richard J. Lawrence, USA
Naszvadi László, Hungary
Roger W. Browne, USA
Bart Clauwens, The Netherlands
Noah Feiler-Poethke, USA
Jonathan Hardy, UK
John S. Kundrat, USA
Vincent Sauvé, USA
Chris Somers, Australia

Jagroop Sahota, USA
Edgar Raab, Germany
Gordon Hogenson, USA
Burebista Dacia, Romania
Christel Hahn, Germany
Robert Angstrom, USA
Norman Chadwick, USA
Harley Orr, USA
Clive Martin-Ross, UK
Alasdair Martin, UK
Marcus Ellspermann, Germany
Bruce Richardson, USA
John Dill, USA
Judith Woollard, Australia
Michael Cyrek, USA
Randall Meyers, Italy
Craig Arend, USA
Onur Cantimur, Turkey
Roland Scheel, France
Murat Isik, Turkey
Markus Hellebrandt, Germany
Mehmet Kara, Turkey
Abhishek Dey Das, India
D. N. Vazquez, USA
Suzan R. Rodenburg, USA
Shuming Zhang, China
Codie Vickers, USA
Elfriede Steiner-Grillmair, Canada
Michael Wember, USA
Fuksz Levente, Romania
Seppo Tuominen, Finland
Marvin C. Katz, USA

Laura Fridley, USA
Michael Christian, USA
Edgar S. Hill, USA
Q. John T. Malone, USA
Michael Bruttel, Switzerland
Eric W. LaFlamme, USA
Robert Diegis, Romania
William S. Jarnagin, USA
Kevin Glaser, USA
JoAnn Arcuri, USA
Attila Csanyi, USA
Pratik Sinha, India
Donald C. Bull, New Zealand
Hans Walhout, The Netherlands
Robyn Stewart, Australia
Tor Johannessen, Norway
Rick Schmidt, USA
Terence Watts, UK
Jody Fulford, USA
Gene Gordon, USA
Monica Veloso Alves, Brazil
Ferdi Prins, South Africa
Adam Hansil, USA
Herbert M. Watson, USA
John Patchett, UK
Jurrie Noordijk, The Netherlands
P.S. Phillips, USA
Martin Gradwell, ns, UK
Sami Murtomäki, Ns, Finland
Anthony Abruzzo, USA
Tim Reed, ns, USA
Daniel Rijo, ns, USA

Ken Couesbouc, ns, France
David L. Harrison, USA
Kees de Boer
Tom Higgins, USA
David Calder Hardy, New Zealand
Jochen Moerman, Belgium
Berend de Boer, New Zealand
Edward E. Rom, USA
Jukka Kinnunen, Finland
Jerome M. Hall, USA
Maria Alvarez, Argentina
Paul Chabot, Canada
Julia, Russia
Amr Malik, Canada
Maureen Bevill, USA
Horst Barwinek, Austria
Lindsay Smith, Australia
Richard DeLano, USA
Stefan Landherr, Australia
Peter Wilson, USA
Gregory Kiser, USA

As one can clearly see by the endorsements, Lerner's thoughts on the Big Bang Theory are shared by many in the scientific community.

"Learner's Endorsements are for his article and not this book"

Most truths are easily discerned, such as the difference between right and wrong, good and evil, while other things that are unclear require research.

"RESEARCH RESEARCH RESEARCH"

After reviewing the evidence, it's clear The Genesis story and the Big Bang Theory cannot be proven. In addition, they escape any relevant truth to support them.

The need for man-kind to explain their beginnings is an age old endeavor that has been driven by curiosity, greed and ego. This mystery may never be revealed, BUT **THE GOOD NEWS IS IT DOESN'T MATTER;** for is it not enough that we are given this gift of life?

Isaiah 45:9 Woe unto him that striveth with his Maker! Let the potsherd *strive* with the potsherds of the earth. Shall the clay say to him that fashioneth it, What makest thou?

Chapter 13

THE EVOLUTION MYTH

Evolution is one of the most bizarre and most defended myths of all time. Taught in schools as though it's factual, it's actually based upon nothing more than unproven conjectures and wild exaggerations.

Also, a favorite among most atheists, evolution is the single most important foothold they have, and one they fully support.

"Evolution is unproved and improvable, we believe it because the only alternative is special creation, which is unthinkable." (Sir Arthur Keith, anthropologist)

"I believe that one day the Darwinian myth will be ranked the greatest deceit in the history of science. When this happens, many people will pose the question, "How did this ever happen?" **(Dr. Soren Lovtrup, Embryologist)**

Evolutionists claim the following as evidence:

Fossil record
Similarities among species
Mutations
Spontaneous generation

Their most convincing argument however comes in the form of a variety of different graphs, and drawings that are far more convincing than anything they could ever possibly prove. By using the power of visual aids, these cleverly designed graphs and drawings add credibility to what otherwise would be a loss cause.

One such drawing is called the *Road to Homo Sapiens*, an illustration which shows an ape that eventually transforms into a man. Known worldwide, this drawing has become one of the most familiar icons in history.

Even though there is not one ounce of proof that this transformation from ape to man ever took place, this illustration is a perfect example of the power of visual aids.

Evolutionist would have you believe that mankind evolved from apes, but rarely do they talk about what apes evolved from, and on down the line to that first one single cell organism that they claim came about from non-living matter. "This is why graphs are so valuable to evolutionist"

Actually Evolutionist would prefer to sit out five different skulls ranging in various sizes and shapes on a table and then try to convince you that the close similarities prove the stages of man's evolution.

They don't divulge two or three of those skulls are nothing more than species that went extinct long ago and have nothing to do with mankind.

> *"We have now the remarkable spectacle that just when many scientific men are agreed that there is no part of the Darwinian system that is of any great influence, and that, as a whole, the theory is not only unproved, but impossible, the ignorant, half-educated masses have acquired the idea that it is to be accepted as a fundamental fact." (Dr. Thomas Dwight, famed professor at Harvard University)*

As part of their science curriculum our children are forced to learn and accept the Big Bang and Evolution as truth, this type of deception is inexcusable!

When children are taught falsehoods such as the Big Bang and Evolution are true, and when God is removed or diminished from their lives, their hope and morals become challenged. The effects are easily seen in the increase of violence, suicides and mass shootings among our children.

"This is how Truth Blindness occurs, and it must be stopped, our children must be taught TRUTH, not conjecture."

> *"Hypothesis [evolution] based on no evidence and irreconcilable with the facts….These classical evolutionary theories are a gross over- simplification of an immensely complex and intricate mass of facts, and it amazes me that they are swallowed so uncritically and readily, and for such a long time, by so many scientists without a murmur of protest." (Sir Ernst Chan, Nobel Prize winner for developing penicillin)*

> *"Scientists who go about teaching that evolution is a fact of life are great con men, and the story they are telling may be the greatest hoax ever. In explaining evolution we do not have one iota of fact.' A tangled mishmash*

of guessing games and figure juggling [Tahmisian called it]."—*The Fresno Bee, August 20, 1959, p. 1-B [quoting T.N. Tahmisian, physiologist for the Atomic Energy Commission].*

Chapter 14

THE FOSSIL RECORD MYTH

Another myth that is used by some evolutionist is Transitional Forms, which they claim exist in the fossil records. "Hypothetically speaking, transitional forms are fossilized images believed to show one type of animal evolving into another type".

> "As by this theory, innumerable transitional forms must have existed. Why do we not find them embedded in the crust of the earth? Why is not all nature in confusion instead of being, as we see them, well defined species?" —*Charles Darwin

According to science there have been five mass extinctions in Earth history. Each time one of these extinctions happened, nearly all known life was destroyed. Therefore, any fossil thought to be a transitional fossil, is likely nothing more than an unknown species that went extinct long ago.

> *Darwin confessed: "There are two or three million species on earth. A sufficient field one might think for observation; but it must be said today that in spite of all the evidence of trained observers, not one change of the species to another is on record." [Life and Letters, vol. 3, p. 25]*

> *"The only competing explanation for the order we all see in the biological world is the notion of special creation." (Dr. Colin Patterson, evolutionist and senior Paleontologist at the British Museum of Natural History, which houses 60 million fossils)*

Chapter 15

SIMILARITY MYTH

Hardly worth mentioning, but some evolutionist claim whenever two different species share similar traits, it's somehow proof of evolution.

Yet it's quite common among different species to share similar traits, such as bone structure, a ribcage, and the number of eyes, ears, legs, and nose just to name a few. **THIS PROVES NOTHING.** Monkeys don't breed with chimpanzees, or gorillas with orangutan's, or any combination thereof. Every animal is of its own kind.

"The pathetic thing about it is that many scientists are trying to prove the

doctrine of evolution, which no science can do." (Dr. Robert A. Millikan, physicist and Nobel Prize winner)

"The theory of evolution is a scientific mistake" Louis Agassiz, quoted in H. Enoch, Evolution or Creation, p. 139. Agassiz was a Harvard University professor and the pioneer in glaciation.

"The reality of human evolution is based on nothing more than a growing intelligence in nutrition, medicine, and medical procedures which has allowed mankind to grow taller, stronger, and live longer"

Chapter 16

MUTATION MYTH

The next part of the evolution myth is Mutations, the only explanation evolutionist have for advance life forms.

It's their belief that life started out from non-living matter, and then through the process of Mutations, life evolved into the advance forms as we know them today.

"In conclusion, evolution is not observable, repeatable, or refutable, and thus does not qualify as either a scientific fact or theory." (Dr. David N. Menton, PhD in Biology from Brown University)

Here's the problem with this part of the myth, Mutations don't happen that often, and when they do they nearly always have a negative effect. Here is a small example of diseases caused by Mutations: Progeria, Uner Tan syndrome, Epidermodysplasia Verruciformis, Severe Combined Immunodeficiency Disorder (SCID), Ectrodactyly, Proteus Syndrome, Marfan Syndrome, Down Syndrome, and Sickle-cell Anaemia, and Cancers.

"The success of Darwinism was accomplished by a decline in scientific integrity." (Dr. W.R. Thompson, world renowned Entomologist)

I believe the following comments made by Professor G.G. Simpson pretty much sums up this Mutation myth.

"Professor G. G. Simpson, a spokesmen for evolution, reports that the mathematical likelihood of getting good evolutionary results would occur only once in 274 billion years! And that would be assuming 100 million individuals reproducing a new generation every day! He concludes by saying: "Obviously ... such a process has played no part whatever in evolution" (The Major Features of Evolution, p. 96).

CHAPTER 17

SPONTANEOUS GENERATION MYTH

Spontaneous Generation: "The first step of the evolution myth, a hypothetical process by which a living organism develops from nonliving matter" the keyword being HYPOTHETICAL.

> *The probability of life originating from accident is comparable to the probability of the unabridged dictionary resulting from an explosion in a printing shop." (Dr. Edwin Conklin, evolutionist and professor of biology at Princeton University)*

Louis Pasteur's 1859 experiment debunking Spontaneous Generation is widely viewed as having settled the debate. In Pasteur's own words he considered spontaneous generation as utter foolishness.

In 1864 Pasteur referring to his experiment said, "Never will the doctrine of spontaneous generation recover from the mortal blow struck by this simple experiment."

> "The chance that higher life forms might have emerged through evolutionary processes is comparable with the chance that a tornado sweeping through a junk yard might assemble a Boeing 747 from the material therein." (Sir Fred Hoyle, Highly respected British astronomer and mathematician)

> "The probability for the chance of formation of the smallest, simplest form of living organism known is 1 to 10-340,000,000. This number is 1 to 10 to the 340 millionth power! The size of this figure is truly staggering, since there is only supposed to be approximately 10-80 (10 to the 80th power) electrons in the whole universe!" (Professor Harold Morowitz)

"One has only to contemplate the magnitude of this task to concede that the spontaneous generation of a living organism is impossible. Yet here we are—as a result, I believe, of spontaneous generation." (Dr. George Wald, Nobel Prize winner of Harvard university, Atheist.) Scientific American, August 1954.

"This is a perfect example of how diehard an Atheist can be"

After Spontaneous Generation was disproven by Pasteur, the term Spontaneous Generation became tainted and eventually took on another name, Abiogenesis, same basic concept just different name.

CHAPTER 18

THE INTELLIGENCE BEHIND DNA

DNA and the intelligence behind it is a nightmare for evolutionist. The following is an article from EveryStudent.com that was broken down so well I thought I'd pass it on.

"DNA in our cells is very similar to an intricate computer program."

In the photo on the left, you see that a computer program is made up of a series of ones and zeros (called binary code). The sequencing and ordering of these ones and zeros is what makes the computer program work properly.

computer programming:

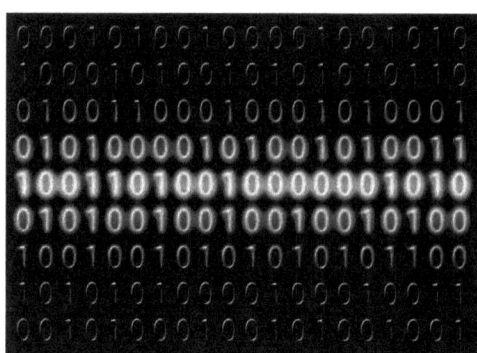 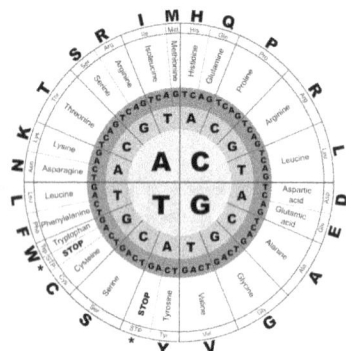

DNA code:

In the same way, DNA is made up of four chemicals, abbreviated as letters A, T, G, and C. Much like the ones and zeros, these letters are arranged in the human cell like this: CGTGTGACTCGCTCCTGAT and so on. The order in which they are arranged instructs the cell's actions.

What is amazing is that within the tiny space in every cell in your body, this code is three billion letters long!!

To grasp the amount of DNA information in one cell, "a live reading of that code at a rate of three letters per second would

take thirty-one years, even if reading continued day and night."

Information such as code is much more complex than the written language. Now consider three billion letters of code all within one small cell.

Evolutionist would have you believe this was possible by the Old Abracadabra technique called a mutation, but as we already discussed, that type of reasoning is best left to the shaman and soothsayers of the world.

Another interesting read on evolution is: (THE EVOLUTION FRAUD) https://theevolutionfraud.blogspot.com/

Chapter 19

GOD MYTHS CONTINUED

As discussed earlier, most everything one knows about God is based upon nothing more than some ancient writings found within the Bible, Torah, and Quran.

In these writings liberties were taken to speak on God's behalf as the ancients portrayed God as someone to be feared, a jealous God, capable of killing and demanding worship.

However, this is far from the truth and a complete opposite of Gods known characteristics and nature.

One example is the flood story of Noah. According to Genesis, only Noah and those on the ark lived through the flood. God supposedly was guilty of killing every baby, every child, every woman and every man on earth, total genocide.

It's not so surprising that many Atheist blame the cruelty found in these ancient stories as their reason for not believing in God.

Although there have been many false stories written about God, unlike atheist there are those that have been able to look beyond the fabrication and deceit of these ancient writings and still believe in God, they are called DEIST.

Deist view these writings as nothing more than ancient stories that in no way represents the TRUE GOD.

The following is a short list of some popular Deist.

George Washington	American President
Thomas Jefferson	American President
James Madison	American President
Abraham Lincoln	American President
Thomas Paine	United States Founding Father
Benjamin Franklin	United States Founding Father

Thomas Alva Edison	American inventor
Jules Verne	Author
Mark Twain	Author
Neil Armstrong	American astronaut
Napoleon Bonaparte	French military leader
Leonardo da Vinci	Painter, Scientist, mathematician
Max Planck	Physicist
Max Born	Physicist and Nobel Prize winner

As Deist this group was blessed with the ability to break free from the traditions of Truth Blindness. By using their God given ability to reason, they were able to truthfully question these ancient writings.

> "SUCH CRUEL STORIES WRITTEN ABOUT GOD ARE UNTRUE. THE TELLTALE SIGN THAT THESE STORIES ARE PHONY FABRICATIONS IS THAT THEY GO AGAINST GOD'S OWN NATURE OF PERFECT LOVE, FORGIVINGNESS, AND MERCY"

When Cain murderer Able, God didn't kill Cain, "no eye for an eye" instead it's written that the Lord set a mark on Cain, lest anyone finding him should kill him. God was actually protecting Cain.

As you'll see, the ancient writers had a hard time keeping things consistent.

One such inconsistency is: 1 John 4:12 "no man hath seen God at any time".

However, in genesis 32:30 Jacob said "I have seen God face to face, and my life is preserved"

And then again in Exodus 24:9-11 God is seen:

[9] Then went up Moses, and Aaron, Nadab, and Abihu, and seventy of the elders of Israel:

[10] And they saw the God of Israel: and there was under his feet as it were a paved work of a sapphire stone, and as it were the body of heaven in his clearness.

[11] And upon the nobles of the children of Israel he laid not his hand: also they saw God, and did eat and drink.

Then again, in Exodus 33:20 the Lord said, Thou canst see my face; for no man shall see me and live.

And once again in Exodus 33:11 "So the Lord spoke to Moses face to face, as a man speaks to his friend"

You would think getting this one fact straight would have been of the utmost importance.

In the story of Sodom and Gomorrah God is accused of killing all the inhabitants for their evilness, but allows Lot to survive who later has sex with both his daughters.

It's quite clear this story wasn't about morality, it was about having the people fear God so they'd succumb to their leaders.

In the book of Exodus God is accused of killing all the firstborn of Egypt. THIS NEVER HAPPENED, thus the reason why no evidence of the exodus has ever been discovered, nor was this ever recorded by the Egyptians.

According to these ancient writings even slavery is permitted by God. In Exodus 21:7 the selling of a daughter into slavery is acceptable. This is just another falsehood, and more proof of mankind speaking on God's behalf, as infinite love doesn't condone slavery.

Numbers 31:1-2 And the Lord spoke to Moses, saying : Take vengeance on the Midianites for the children of Israel.

Numbers 31:7 And they warred against the Midianites, just as the Lord commanded Moses, and they killed all the males.

Numbers 31:17 Now therefore, kill every male among the little ones {male children}, and kill every woman who has known a man intimately.

Deuteronomy 20:13 "And when the Lord your God delivers it into your hands, you shall strike every male in it with the edge of the sword"

Deuteronomy 20:16 "but of the cities of these people which the Lord your God gives you as an inheritance, you shall let nothing that breaths remain alive"

These verses from Numbers and Deuteronomy are a perfect example of those that use God's name to justify their merciless actions. "This is so very typical of extreme religious radicals"

"MARK 7:7 "Howbeit in vain do they worship me, teaching for doctrines the commandments of men"

Here is more fabrication:

Exodus 34:14 "For you shall worship no other god, for the Lord, whose name is Jealous, is a jealous God"

However, when we go to Isaiah 42:8 God says: "I am the Lord, that is my name" Obviously another contradiction.

Deuteronomy 4:24 "The LORD thy God is a consuming fire, even a jealous God"

Deuteronomy 6:15 "(for the LORD thy God is a jealous God among you) lest the anger of the LORD thy God be kindled against thee, and destroy thee from off the face of the earth"

Joshua 24:19 "for he is an holy God; he is a jealous God"

Jealousy is ENVY, RESENTFULNESS, SPITE, HATRED, AND EVIL. To say that Gods name is JEALOUS is totally RIDICULOUS; to accuse God of being jealous is even more RIDICULOUS.

> **"JEALOUSY IS A CHARACTERISTIC THAT DOESN'T EXIST IN GODS NATURE"**

These are just a few small examples of the God myths and fabrications found within the ancient writings of the Bible, Torah, and Quran.

These accusations accusing God of such brutal demented acts are inexcusable.

> "One must understand that acts of violence and anger is contrary to Gods perfect nature"

Another common myth is that God is a narcissist demanding worship; however, nowhere in the ancient writings does it say,

"I the Lord God demand worship" or "thus says the Lord your God, worship me".

You MUST understand PERFECT LOVE is a part of God's nature. God loves you and only wants the best for you; God tries to protect you from worshipping false idols/lies because God knows it'll lead you down a wicked and treacherous road.

God only wants to enrich your life, but a relationship is a two-way street and you have free will, so it's your choice.

CHAPTER 20

THE ONE TRUE GOD

After reading the Old Testament it's not surprising that so many come away thinking of God as a jealous, worship demanding barbarian that must be feared.

IT'S TIME TO SET THE RECORD STRAIGHT!

GOD IS GOOD (THIS MEANS THERE IS NO BAD, AND WHERE THERE IS NO BAD THERE IS PERFECTION)

GOD IS PERFECT

GOD HAS INFINITE LOVE

GOD HAS INFINITE UNDERSTANDING

GOD HAS INFINITE HOPE

GOD HAS INFINITE PEACE

GOD HAS INFINITE JOY

GOD HAS INFINITE COMPASSION

GOD HAS INFINITE MERCY

These are only some of the wonderful characteristics of OUR GOD, THE ONE AND ONLY TRUE GOD. ANYTHING TO THE CONTRARY IS NOT OF GODS NATURE.

One should keep in mind The Ancients were from a time when things such as animal sacrifices and barbarism was common place. Therefore, you'll see it reflected in their writings concerning God as well, and thus God is being continually demonized within their writings.

The vicious animal sacrifices, the brutal killings, the genocide of the earth, none of these were of God.

God's love for us is infinite, beyond anything we can imagine, a love that ascends all else.

Chapter 21

NEW TESTAMENT CONTRADICTIONS

Because contradictions can be subject to the reader's discretion, based on how literal one may view them, I'll continue to discuss only the more pertinent and obvious ones.

If you are interested in New Testament or Old Testament contradictions, many can easily be found online.

Below is a short list of New Testament contradictions that I personally consider outright and obvious contradictions.

Matthew 1:16 says Jacob was Joseph's father

Luke 3:23 says Heli was Joseph's father

Matthew 1:25 He was named Jesus

Matthew 1:23 According to Isaiah he was supposed to be named Immanuel

Matthew 4:5-8 The devil took Jesus to the pinnacle, and then to the mountain top.

Luke 4:5-9 The devil takes Jesus to the mountain top first, and then to the pinnacle. "Also during this time of temptation I'm curious who is recording everything that is being said"

Mark 6:53 After feeding the multitude Jesus went to Gennesaret.

John 6:53 They went to Capernaum.

Matthew 5:1 The sermon on the mount took place on a mountain.

Luke 6:17 The sermon took place on a plain.

Matthew 6:9 Jesus teaches the multitude the Lord's prayer on the mount.

Luke 11:1 Jesus teaches only the disciples the Lord's prayer. "Apparently they weren't paying attention on the mount"

Romans 3:10 There is none righteous.

Matthew 25:46 And these shall go away into everlasting punishment: but the righteous into life eternal. "But Romans says none is righteous"

James 1:13-15 Let no man say when he is tempted, I am tempted of God: for God cannot be tempted with evil, neither tempted he any man:

And yet in the Lord's prayer Jesus is asking God to LEAD US NOT INTO TEMPTATION. And how about poor Job that got worked over when god was trying to settle a disagreement with Satan.

First Timothy 5:8 But if any provide not for his own, and specially for those of his own house, he hath denied the faith, and is worse than an infidel.

Luke 12:22 Jesus said unto his disciples, Therefore I say unto you, Take no thought for your life, what ye shall eat; neither for the body, what ye shall put on. (I agree with Genesis 3:19, for it is written: In the sweat of thy face shalt thou eat bread).

Mark 6:8-9 When Jesus sends out his disciples he commands them to only take sandals and a staff.

Matthew 10:10 When Jesus sends out his disciples he commands them **NOT** to take sandals or a staff.

Matthew 26:30-34 At the Mount of Olives Jesus told Peter he would deny him.

Luke 22:34 At the Passover supper Jesus told Peter he would deny him.

Matthew 27:28 Jesus was given a scarlet robe.

Mark 15:17 Jesus was given a purple robe

Matthew 27:37 The sign on the cross said "This is Jesus the King of the Jews"

Mark 15:26 The sign read "The King of the Jews"

John 19:19-20 The sign read "Jesus of Nazareth, the King of the Jews"

With all the drama at the time on what should be written on the sign, you would think there would be some agreement on what was actually written.

Matthew 27:46 The last words of Jesus: "My God, my God, why have you forsaken me?"

Luke 23:46 "Father into your hands I commend my spirit"

John 19:19 "It is finished" **THREE PEOPLE, THREE DIFFERENT STORIES.**

Matthew 28:1-2 Mary Magdalene and the other Mary go to the tomb of Jesus. There was a great earthquake and an angel of the Lord descended from heaven, and rolled back the stone from the door.

Mark 16:1-5 Mary Magdalene and Mary the mother of James, and Salome came to the tomb. The stone was rolled away "no earthquake, no angel" so they entered the tomb, and there they saw a young man clothed in a long white robe.

Luke 24:1-4 Certain other women went to the tomb, they found the stone rolled away. They went in but didn't find the body of Jesus. They were troubled but behold two men stood by them in shinning garments.

John 20:1-2 Mary Magdalene alone goes to the tomb and finds the stone rolled away, so she runs back to the disciples and tells them Jesus has been taken away from the tomb.

Here we have four totally different stories about the tomb of Jesus being visited, each contradicting the other.

Matthew 27:44 Both thieves mocked Jesus.

Luke 23:39-41 One of the two thieves stood up for Jesus.

Mark 3:29 Blasphemy the Holy Spirit is unforgivable.

1st John 1:9 If you confess your sins they will be forgiven.

Luke 24:50-51 The ascension happened at Bethany.

Mark 16:14-19 The ascension happened while the disciples were seated together.

Acts 1:9-12 The ascension happened at Mount Olivet.

"You would think they'd get this one right"

John 8:14 Jesus says: if he bears witness to himself, his testimony is true.

John 5:31 Jesus says: If I bear witness of myself, my witness is not true.

"Which is it?"

Ephesians 4:28 Paul said: Let him who stole, steal no more.

2 Corinthians 11:8 Paul said: I robbed other churches, taking wages from them to minister to you.

I guess Paul needed the money.

Acts 9:7 When Saul came near Damascus the men that journeyed with him heard a voice but saw no one.

Acts 22:9 Tells a different story, saying the men saw a light and heard nothing.

Chapter 22

THE WORSHIPPING OF JESUS

WORSHIP: To regard with great or extravagant respect, honor, or devotion, praying to, or bowing down on knees to.

Whenever you worship someone or something, it becomes your god. Therefore, if you are worshipping Jesus you are making him your god, or on the same level as the **ONE TRUE GOD.**

So is it all right to worship Jesus or not, let's see what Jesus himself says about worship.

Luke 4:8 "And Jesus answered and said unto him, Get thee behind me, Satan: for it is written, Thou shalt worship the Lord thy God, and him ONLY shalt thou serve."

In this verse Jesus says VERY CLEARLY! "Thou shalt worship the Lord thy God, and him ONLY shalt thou serve"

Jesus himself is saying it's wrong to worship or serve anyone other than God, and yet people praise, and exalt Jesus, contrary to what he himself said to do.

In addition, anyone that worships Jesus is also breaking the first and second commandment: "You shall have no other gods before Me" and "You shall not bow down to them nor serve them"

And yet there are people that worship him by naming their churches in his honor. They sing praises in his name, and many churches even have statues of his supposed likeness.

It seems that no matter what church you go to the theme is about Jesus, not God. Then if we take it one step further, in the Catholic Church they honor Mary the mother of Jesus. They may say they don't worship her, but paying tribute and honor to her is the definition of worship.

Man-made traditions and rituals continue to lead us further and further from God, this must stop.

Chapter 23

THE TRINITY MYTH

"In the eyes of Sir Isaac Newton, worshipping Christ as God was idolatry, to him the fundamental sin"

As for the Trinity or those that believe Jesus was somehow God in the flesh, let's consider the following.

If Jesus was indeed God or the same as God, then to whom was Jesus always praying to and preaching about, surely he wouldn't be praying to himself.

When Jesus was baptized by John and a voice from heaven, said, "This is my beloved Son, in whom I am well pleased" it clearly shows two different and separate identities, in **TWO DIFFERENT LOCATIONS.**

In the Garden of Gethsemane, Jesus is praying to God; Luke 22:39 "My Father, if it is possible, may this cup be taken from me. Yet not as I will, but as you will."

In this verse Jesus is clearly **PLEADING WITH GOD TO STOP WHAT WAS ABOUT TO HAPPEN. This** indicates **TWO DISTINCT INDIVIDUALS.**

Then Jesus says: **"YET NOT AS I WILL, BUT AS YOU WILL"** here there are **TWO DIFFERENT WILLS,** Jesus' will and God's will, thus **TWO DIFFERENT INDIVIDUALS.**

"On another note, how is it possible there is always a writer on the spot to record everything being said word for word. In this particular case the disciples are all asleep and Jesus is praying alone"

Mark 16:19 "So then, after the Lord had spoken to them, He was received up into heaven, and sat down at the **RIGHT HAND OF GOD."** Jesus sat at the **RIGHT HAND** of God, **THE RIGHT HAND.......THUS SHOWING TWO INDIVIDUALS.**

Mark 13:32 "But of that day and that hour knoweth no man, no, not the angels which are in heaven, neither the Son, but the Father" In this verse Jesus is telling his disciples about the end of days, note Jesus himself says that **NO ONE, NEITHER THE SON** knows when that day will come, no one but the **FATHER**. Again this is showing **TWO individual!**

Matthew 27:46 Jesus calls out "My God, my God, why have you forsaken me" If Jesus and God were actually one, then this verse would make zero sense.

Now let's look to see what else Jesus himself says on this matter. Luke 18:18-19; **[18]And a certain ruler asked him, saying, Good Master, what shall I do to inherit eternal life?**

[19] And Jesus said unto him, Why callest thou me good? none is good, save one, that is, God.

In this verse Jesus is REBUKING the man for calling him GOOD, as he proclaims that GOD AND ONLY GOD IS GOOD. (not good as good, better, best, but GOOD as in no bad is present, in other words PERFECT)

This passage unquestionably established the major difference between God and Jesus. **IN HIS OWN WORDS JESUS** made it perfectly clear that **HE IS NOT GOOD**, and that **ONLY GOD IS GOOD/PERFECT!**

"THERE IS NO TRINITY, WHAT MORE PROOF DOES ONE NEED"

BASED UPON THE WORDS JESUS HIMSELF SPOKE, THERE IS DEFINITELY NO TRINITY, AND JESUS ISN'T SECRETLY GOD IN DISGUISE.

Chapter 24

REVEALING THE ANTICHRIST

PLEASE BE ADVISED: We live in a matrix of **TRUTH BLINDNESS**, if you jumped to this chapter without reading the prior chapters first, it could be detrimental and confusing. If you truly desire **TRUTH**, if you're seeking more, please read the **FORWARD** then start from the beginning with chapter 1.

WARNING: THE KNOWING OF GREAT TRUTHS COME GREAT RESPONSIBILITIES

This revealing is sure to be upsetting for a lot of Christians, but it's time this TRUTH is revealed.

Simply put no one fits the description of an antichrist better than Jesus himself. No other has so successfully stolen God's glory, elevating himself as being God or Gods equal, and being worshipped and praised.

In addition, no other has convinced so many that he, **NOT GOD**, is their savior.

"Matthew 24:24 For there shall arise false Christs, and false prophets, and **SHALL SHOW GREAT SIGNS AND WONDERS;** insomuch that, if it were possible, *THEY SHALL DECEIVE THE VERY ELECT*"

Jesus was a master of deflecting and avoiding straight talk, often times using parables as cover. However, because of his narcissistic nature, "he enjoyed talking about himself" he exposed himself for who he really is.

John 5:31 If I bear witness of myself, my witness is not true.

John 8:14 Jesus answered and said unto them, Though I bear record of myself, *yet* my record is true:

"John 7:18 He that speaketh of himself seeketh his own glory"

Because people believe in the Jesus Savior myth for **NO OTHER REASON THAN IT'S WRITTEN IN THE BIBLE**, we'll use the same source, the Bible, as evidence against this myth. Going one step further we'll also use the exact words stated by Jesus himself as told in the King James Version of the Bible.

We know throughout the New Testament Jesus is referred to as Lord and Savior, however, let us see what the Old Testament has to say.

According to Isaiah 42:8 God says: "I am the Lord, that is my name; And My glory I will not give to another"

Seeing how lying isn't a characteristic of God, this means exactly what it says, that God isn't giving Gods glory to another, this would include Jesus.

In Isaiah 43:11 God says: "I, even I, am the Lord, And besides Me there is no savior"

In this verse God makes it **PERFECTLY CLEAR**, that God is the **ONLY SAVIOR** there is, **THERE IS NO ONE ELSE.**

Isaiah 43:25 God says: *"I, even I, am He who blots out your transgressions for my own sake: And I will not remember your sins"*

This is a very important verse for those that believe God is incapable of forgiving us of our sins.

It also means that Jesus dying on the cross for our sins was nothing more than pure fabrication.

"BUT WHAT AN EXCELLENT WAY FOR THE ANTICHRIST TO WIN THE PEOPLES TRUST!"

(Sacrifices whether human or animal are synonymous with the ancient's way of life, and in no way had anything to do with God)

Isaiah 45:5 God says: "I am the Lord, and there is no other: There is no God besides Me"

Isaiah 45:6 God says: "That they may know from the rising of the sun to its setting: That there is none besides Me, I am the Lord, and there is no other"

In these two verses God says there is no other LORD.

Isaiah 45:21 God says: "And there is no other God besides Me, A just God and a Savior: There is none besides Me"

Here Again God claims to be the Savior, and says there is none other.

Isaiah 45:22 God says: "Look to Me, and be saved, All you ends of the earth! For I am God, and there is no other"

Isaiah 46:5 God says: "To whom will you liken Me, and make Me equal and compare Me, that we should be alike?"

Isaiah 46:9 God says: "Remember the former things of old, For I am God, and there is no other: I am God, and there is none like me"

"The Old Testament is undeniably clear on this matter; GOD and GOD ONLY is our LORD and SAVIOR"

Many Christians will disregard these obvious facts and still defend the New Testament. They will argue that the Old Testament is no longer valid (however, they don't mind saying it's the infallible word or inspired word of God) and that Jesus dying on the cross changed everything.

Whatever excuses the Christian community wants to use, the facts remain irrefutable, the Old Testament says God is Lord and Savior, and the New Testament claims Jesus is Lord and Savior, these are the undeniable true facts as stated in the bible.

Let's stay on track with what we know is the truth and move forward.

Christians will also argue that Jesus died on the cross for our sins, however, in Isaiah 43:25 God says: "I, EVEN I, AM HE WHO BLOTS OUT YOUR TRANSGRESSIONS FOR MY OWN SAKE: AND I WILL NOT REMEMBER YOUR SINS"

This verse unmistakably states that God will forgive us our sins, and with that being said, one must also remember **GOD IS PERFECT IN GRACE, MERCY, AND FORGIVENESS.**

Here are a couple of things that you should know; one is that God doesn't need the help of Jesus or anyone else, and second, God is more than capable of forgiving us our sins.

In the New Testament we find where Jesus time after time compares himself to God.

John 14:8-9 Philip said to Him, "Lord, show us the Father, and it is enough for us." 9 Jesus said to him, "Have I been so long with you, and yet you have not come to know Me, Philip? He who has seen Me has seen the Father; how can you say, 'Show us the Father '?

John 10:30 "I and the Father are one."

However, Isaiah 46:5 God says: "To whom will you liken Me, and make Me equal and compare Me, that we should be alike?"

In John 14:6 Jesus said : "I am the way, and the truth, and the life; no one comes to the Father but through Me."

Here we find Jesus using misdirection by making himself the middleman between humankind and God. This is the exact type of deception and self glorifying that one would expect from the antichrist!

If the bible is indeed infallible as Christians confess it to be, then they must concede that the New Testament contradicts what GOD says in the Old Testament.

The evidence from the Old Testament plainly states time and time again that God and God only is our Lord and Savior, with that being said, *anyone else claiming to be our Lord and Savior is an antichrist.*

Therefore, unless you are willing to take the word of the New Testament Jesus, "Who may never existed" over the spoken word of God in the Old Testament, then Jesus is indeed an antichrist.

Even though the evidence is INDISPUTABLE, many will never let go of their manmade doctrine of Jesus.

"Humankind has always preferred to worship a god made in their own image"

"The things of God aren't taught by man, they are revealed by God and God only. Such are the truths written in this book, they too will only be revealed to whom God chooses"

Don't be dismayed; what we see from Jesus is what we've seen from a lot of people of religion, the Jim Jones of the world. They first start out innocent and humble glorifying God, but as their own celebrity grows so does their ego's. Soon they become drunk on their own self-righteousness and exalt themselves to a godlike stature.

This could be why Jesus cried out with a loud voice at the end: MARK 15:34 "My God, My God, why have You forsaken Me"

In that verse we also see Jesus referring to God as God not Father, as though he had just remembered his place.

The following verse speaks volumes about Jesus. Luke 14:26 "If any *man* come to me, and hate not his father, and mother, and wife, and children, and brethren, and sisters, yea, and his own life also, he cannot be my disciple"

Does this sound like a savior or a jealous narcissist that doesn't want you to love the other people in your life?

In view of the TRUTH, we can't honestly say with all certainty that such a person as Jesus ever really existed, the evidence is somewhat dubious, but regardless the damage is done and continues.

> *"The priests of the present day, profess to believe it. They gain their living by it, and they exclaim against something they call infidelity. I will define what it is. HE THAT BELIEVES IN THE STORY OF CHRIST IS AN INFIDEL TO GOD"*
>
> **THOMAS PAINE**

Chapter 25

THIS IS WHAT WE DO KNOW

Liberties were taken in the Old Testament to damage God's reputation, for the most part having God appear to be jealous, ruthless, unforgiving, and a quick tempered bully.

Then all of a sudden a New Testament comes along, (this really should have been the tipoff something wasn't right) with it a new character that claims to be the **NEW SAVIOR** of the people, **"NOT GOD"**. In the end he earns the trust of the people, and they praise and worship him like God, **THE ANTICHRIST'S ULTIMATE GOAL**.

Because evil is always at hand, the evidence would suggest these ancient writings, "both the Old and New Testament" were purposely tainted. Not only are they both full of contradictions, they're very deceptive, as they both lead the people away from the ONE TRUE GOD and right into the arms of the Antichrist. Just like sheep to the slaughter.

Chapter 26

THE LARGEST HOAX IN THE HISTORY OF THE WORLD

With more than 2 billion current believers, or roughly one-third of the world's population, Christianity is the largest religion in the world, **AND THE BIGGEST HOAX OF ALL TIME.**

Without Jesus as the anchor of Christianity it can no longer survive. Many of the **TRUTH BLIND** will continue to follow the traditions for a time, but eventually it will fall to **TRUTH**. But for now it's important to understand how Christianity was able to deceive so many.

The answer to that question starts with the establishment of Christianity, because from that point on it became heresy to question it or the church.

Because the deterrent for heresy was flogging, imprisonment, or death, Christianity went basically unchecked and unchallenged.

So strong are the bonds of religion that a mere 260 years ago so-called witches were still being burned at the stake or executed in other ways, as Christians believed they were doing God's will. Exodus 22:18 "thou shalt not suffer a witch to live"

Even after 1750 years of Christian barbarism, generations after generation are still being taught that Jesus is the savior of the world, and again few dare to question it.

Many deterrents are still being used to keep Christians under the influence of the church, one such deterrent is the fear of burning in hell for eternity for not confessing Jesus as one's savior. This one deterrent alone has probably brought more people into the hands of the antichrist than anything else. "God is infinite in **LOVE** and **FORGIVINGNESS**, not in **HATE** and **REVENGE**."

After nearly 2000 years of Jesus being programmed into the minds of society, together with the fear of heresy and burning in hell for eternity, it's not that surprising so many **STILL SUFFER FROM TRUTH BLINDNESS!!**

Chapter 27

FREE WILL

"EACH OF US ARE INDIVIDUALS, UNIQUE, AND DISTINCTIVE BECAUSE WE HAVE FREE WILL. WITHOUT FREE WILL WE WOULD NOT BE INDIVIDUALS, WE WOULD BE NOTHING MORE THAN PROGRAMMED ROBOTS"

God has blessed us with **FREE WILL**, allowing us to make our own choices for better or worse, **GOOD OR EVIL**.

Free Will however comes with a stipulation attached, CONSEQUENCES. Which simply means you can be held accountable for the choices you make.

Quick example: You choose to drive yourself home after having some drinks with a friend, and on your way home you get pulled over by the police and taken to jail.

The consequences for your bad choices include a traffic violation, a fine, and jail. In addition, your drinking got you fired from your job, your spouse is all upset and worried, your insurance company dropped you, and you have no idea what you're going to do next, CONSEQUENCES.

This is life, and this is the reality of life, there are no take backs, and seldom any second chances. Each of us **WILL** eventually be held accountable for the choices we make.

CONSEQUENCES CONSEQUENCES CONSEQUENCES

"YOU WILL FIND LIFE IS MUCH MORE ENJOYABLE WHEN YOU MAKE GOOD CHOICES"

Here is another example:

A suicide bomber goes into a busy store, sets a bomb off that kills him and 10 other people.

In this example we have only one person making a bad choice, however, others will suffer the effects.

This is the type of scenario some people blame for their disbelief in God, claiming if God really existed God would never let this happen.

What these naysayers fail to understand is that the bomber also has FREE WILL, and had God intervened against the bombers FREE WILL, that would violate the FREE WILL process.

> *"FREE WILL IS HAVING THE OPTION TO CHOOSE BAD AS WELL AS GOOD. TAKE AWAY EITHER OPTION AND WE NO LONGER HAVE FREE WILL"*

FREE WILL is a bit more involved, but in short this is the reason why it appears GOD DOESN'T INTERFER. (Never forget though that God can do as God pleases)

What must be understood is that God gave you FREE WILL because GOD LOVES YOU. God wants you to choose good, but not because you're being forced or programmed, but because you want to. And if and when you start a relationship with God, you will do so of your own Free Will, and not because you were programmed that way.

> "HAVING TO ACCEPT THE BAD WITH THE GOOD, THIS IS THE PRICE WE PAY FOR FREE WILL AND INDIVIDUALISM"

It's clear that we live in a world of Free Will, with that being said, why is God unfairly blamed whenever something terrible happens.

We are not perfect beings, we have tainted ourselves with pollution and sin of our own making. We pass on our defects, in the form of cancer, diabetes, mental illness, disease and the list goes on. Not only have we infected ourselves, we've infected our planet, our water, and the air we breathe. We reek-havoc on ourselves and blame God for letting it happen. It's time that man-kind stands accountable for their own choices and stop blaming God.

Because we have tainted ourselves and our planet with toxic poisons of all kinds, there are no guarantees in childbirth, yet if a child is born with a deformity, dies of complications or disease, people want to blame God; However, it was the parent's choice to have children, they're the ones that chose to take the risk.

An atheist once asked me, if there is a God then why are innocent Ethiopian children born in such poverty? Well, the truth is it doesn't matter whether they're poor Ethiopians or poor Americans, they were born into the conditions that we the people have made for them.

"WE SUFFER AT THE HAND OF MAN-KIND, NOT GOD"

We can never blame God for our own misfortunes, for God has given us the ability to feed the hungry, to house the homeless, care for the sick, educate the masses, and to clean our air and water.

Chapter 28

GODS WILL

"LOVE AND TRUST GOD COMPLETELY, FOR ONLY GOD IS WORTHY OF WORSHIP"

One can't begin to know the infinite Will of God, yet because of Gods infinite love we can surmise that God desires the following for us:

THAT WE SHOULD,

   Love each other.

Be honest and truthful.

Show compassion and be merciful.

Be peaceful and understanding.

Work hard and be generous to the less fortunate.

Be helpful and respectful to everyone.

Keeping The Ten Commandments as listed should also be included.

1. *You shall have no other gods before you:* **There is only one true God, our creator.** *Let no one or anything come between you and God!*

2. *You shall have no idols:* **Simply put, don't value THINGS to the point you become obsessed with them. So many have fallen short of a TRUE relationship with God by attaching themselves to idols, false doctrines, and false prophets, beware of those that set snares to trap you.**

3. *You Shall Not Take Our Lord God's Name In Vain:* **We shouldn't loosely**

swear using God's name however, it goes much deeper so let's clarify.

Whenever someone makes the statement; God said this or God said that, and God didn't say it, they're taking the Lord's name in vain. So be warned, before throwing God's name out there, think twice!

4. *Keep the Sabbath Day:* No one but God and possibly Gods chosen knows when the first day was, therefore, it's impossible for us to say which day is the 7th day of the week. If we look at our current calendar then actually Saturday is the last day of each week, not Sunday which is traditional for many.

I don't think God actually needed to rest as told in Genesis, but I do think it makes good sense for us to take at least one day a week to rest from our labors and be with our families, and be mindful of all God has done. Again, it doesn't matter which day you choose.

5. *Honor your father and your mother:* Yes, you should treat your father and mother with respect; however, I would

believe God would have us to treat everyone with respect and compassion. *The Golden Rule should apply here;* we should treat others in a manner in which we would like to be treated. If the people of the world could ever master the Golden Rule, what a paradise we would have.

6. *You Shall Not Murder "Suicide is Murder":* God is a God of perfect love not hate, those that kill in the name of God will not be found guiltless. **BEWARE** and do not be deceived by lies and promises of grandeur.

7. *You Shall Not Commit Adultery:* When one enters into marriage they take a sacred oath, an oath that should not be made with doubt. Don't enter into marriage with someone you know is wrong, these relationships seldom stand the test of time.

   Don't marry for convenience sake, or because you feel obligated. It's so important that you wait for your True Love, the person you know without a doubt that you want to spend the rest of your life with.

Keep in mind, **TRUE LOVE is a Two-way street, therefore your partner MUST FEEL THE SAME about you. If you detect your partner doesn't feel the same about you, regardless of how much it hurts, let them go. Sometimes life requires you to be stronger than you want to be, but True Love is worth the wait. SETTLE FOR NOTHING LESS.**

8. *You shall not steal:* **Not only should you not take another's property; you should not steal their dignity, or self-respect by ridicule, mockery or bullying.**

9. *You shall not (lie) bear false witness against your neighbor:* **In this commandment the word neighbor means everyone. (we are all neighbors/brothers and sisters)**

10. *You shall not covet:* **Always be content and thankful for everything you have been blessed with. You will never have inner peace or joy if you're envious of others.**

Chapter 29

YOUR PURPOSE

People often confuse **PURPOSE** with **OCCUPATION**, but the two are not the same. A person's **OCCUPATION** is how they choose to earn a living, while everyone's **PURPOSE** should be the same; **SERVE GOD**. For there's no greater purpose or honor in life than serving God and spreading God's love.

LOVE IS THE GREATEST GIFT GOD HAS GIVEN US, WHICH MEANS IT'S THE GREATESS GIFT THAT WE CAN GIVE.

"Do all things unto others, as you would want God to do them unto you"

When you feel your life has been turned upside down, and you're in need of a smile, there's no easier way to regain your balance than to spread God's love. **GET OFF THE PITY WAGON, GET UP AND GO REACH OUT TO SOMEONE.** Visit a sick friend, lend your neighbor a hand, help your parents/ children/ etc, make a gift for someone, learn an instrument, **DO SOMETHING!**

If you feel empty, **SPREAD GODS LOVE.**

If you feel lost, **SPREAD GODS LOVE.**

If you feel lacking, **SPREAD GODS LOVE.**

If you feel there's something missing, **SPREAD GODS LOVE.**

If you feel unloved, **SPREAD GODS LOVE.**

If you feel no one understands you, **SPREAD GODS LOVE.**

If you're hurting inside, **SPREAD GODS LOVE.**

Give your mind a break, **SPREAD GODS LOVE.**

If you are bored, **SPREAD GODS LOVE**

Chapter 30

LOVE – JOY – HOPE AND SUICIDE

Without God's love there is no hope, and without hope there is no joy. "Because of FREE WILL, the amount of love you feel depends on you."

Many people believe that all their problems would be solved if only they were wealthy, but wealth has nothing to do with God's love. Wealthy people get just as depressed as everyone else, and they also commit suicide as well.

We wonder how can this be, for instance, how can a celebrity that has fame, fortune, and everything they could ever want, choose death over life? The answer is, **HOPELESSNESS.**

When a person feels hopeless, life itself becomes their hell. Once a person reaches this stage, suicide becomes their answer to ending the torment.

Because suicide affects so many people, "rich and poor" we'll address it further.

For those that are deeply depressed it's important to note, that the use of drugs and/or alcohol, regardless of the amounts can easily attribute to someone doing something they may otherwise not do.

Self-medicating is never the answer, **IT WILL ONLY COMPOUND YOUR SITUATION.** When a person is teetering or contemplating suicide, self-medicating can easily push a person past the danger zone. If you or someone you know is feeling depressed and hopeless, see a doctor immediately!

Depression can be physical, **YES PHYSICAL !!** You may have a brain tumor or a vitamin deficiency. If your doctor doesn't find anything physically wrong, then see a **PSYCHIATRIST** that specializes in the diagnosis and treatment of **DEPRESSION**, odds are you have a Serotonin Deficiency. Serotonin is a chemical that is manufactured in the brain, it influences either directly or indirectly brain cells related to mood, sexual desire and function, appetite, sleep, memory and learning, temperature regulation, and some social behavior.

If you suffer from depression or panic attacks, don't see a Medical Doctor, see a **PSYCHIATRIST**. Psychiatrists don't mend broken bones or do surgeries, and Medical Doctors shouldn't treat Psychological Disorders. In addition, **DON'T DELAY**, these types of disorders will continue to get worse over time, the sooner you get treatment the better !!!!

It may take several tries before the right combination of drugs and dosages are found that best works for you, so stay with it.

Once the right medication(s) is found and you're feeling all better you may feel tempted to quit using your medicine, **DON'T**, it's a common mistake that many make.

For starters, the odds are almost 100% your depression will come back, and more than likely it'll be **WORSE THAN BEFORE**.

Also, with these types of drugs there's no guarantee that the medication that once worked will still be effective. So whatever you do, don't stop taking your medication!

One last word on suicide; THOU SHALL NOT MURDER, also pertains to suicide. Killing is killing, and it makes no different if you kill yourself, or someone else.

Atheist enjoy the argument, SHOW ME GOD, and yet our very existence depends on Gods' Love-Joy-Hope, three things that none of us can physically see, touch, smell, hear, or taste.

There's no doubt, without Gods Love-Joy-Hope, life is truly meaningless and irrelevant, yet these unseen, unheard, untouchable forces are the essence of our being and survival.

If love-joy-hope need not be seen, heard, or touched to be believed, how then can one question the existence of God from whence they come.

Chapter 31

PRAYER

Prayer isn't the I NEED I WANT hotline, nor does one need to tell God of their needs, as God knows your needs better than you.

"GOD MAY NOT GIVE YOU WHAT YOU WANT, BUT GOD WILL GIVE YOU WHAT YOU NEED"

Prayer should be more about giving thanks and showing a sincere appreciation for all that God does in your life.

When praying you should ask for compassion, understanding, wisdom, patience, and forgivingness. These are the things that you should wear as armore.

Prayer Is Personal

There has been much talk and concern about prayer being banned in our schools and in the workplace; this should be of no concern because prayer is **PERSONAL**.

Prayer is a private time between you and God, therefore don't put your praying on display, such as before one eats in public.

PRAYER SHOULD NEVER BE A SPECTACLE FOR PUBLIC DISPLAY. *

Although I don't believe everything written in the New Testament, I do agree with the following verses from Matthew 6:5-6.

"When you pray, you are not to be like the hypocrites; for they love to stand and pray in the synagogues and on the street corners so that they may be seen by men. Truly I say to you, they have their reward in full. But you, when you pray, go into your inner room, close your door and pray to your Father who is in secret, and your Father who sees what is done in secret will reward you"

(This should not be confused with group prayer*)

*Group prayer is where a group of people have gathered together, and then as a whole they pray and give thanks to God.

Make no mistake, it's all right to pour your heart out to God, especially if you're hurting, but as your faith advances you'll find no need to remind God of the obvious, instead you will rejoice in the wonder of God's love.

Chapter 32

LIFE AFTER DEATH

For thousands of years, the use of Heaven and Hell has been religions tool of choice, one that has been very convincing and has worked quite well for the church.

The use of Heaven and Hell helps to maintain church attendance, tithing, and control.

But how is it that the homeless and hungry go without, while the major churches are raking in vast amounts of money.

For example: *Pastor Kenneth Copeland has a net worth of $760 Million; He runs Kenneth Copeland Ministries. His ministry's

1,500-acre campus is a half-hour drive from Fort Worth includes a church, a private airstrip, a hangar for the ministry's $17.5 million jet and other aircraft, and a $6 million church owned lakefront mansion.

*ETINSIDE April 2019

This is just one example, there are many church leaders with a net worth in the MILLIONS !!!!

Consider for yourself what would be more pleasing to God; that you should give contributions to a millionaire preacher, or give instead to the homeless and hungry. How can one be confused as to God's will in this matter.

If there was no so-called REWARD, no promise of eternity in paradise, and no fear of burning in hell, I wonder how many Christians and Muslims would still be believers.

If there is no tomorrow, is it not enough that God has given us the gift of life, for whatever amount of time it may be for. Would one love God any less if there's no paradise?

If one's love and loyalty for God is based solely on a life in paradise, that isn't love, **THAT'S A BUSINESS TRANSACTION.**

"ONE'S LOVE FOR GOD SHOULD BE THE SAME WHETHER THERE'S LIFE AFTER DEATH OR NOT"

MY PERSONAL THOUGHTS

My personal view is base on the fact that we are **ENERGY BEINGS**, and as such, I contend that our spirit is **A PURER FORM OF ENERGY.**

In physics, the Law of Conservation of Energy states; "Energy can be neither created nor destroyed, but it can change form"

As such this would mean our spirit energy can't be destroyed, and life would continue on after our earthly bodies expire.

"Knowing that there is Life After Death seems instinctive"

There has been many Life After Death experiences documented, and though they may not be proof positive for life after death, it's hard to totally discount them all.

Then there are times of déjà vu where my intuition whispers the word reincarnation, and the possibility that our spirit may return again and again upon this earth until we finally reach a stage of enlightenment, a stage of spiritual growth that is beyond the earthly body.

FOR THOSE THAT HAVE BEEN BLESSED TO GLIMPSE A LITTLE BIT OF PARADISE HERE ON EARTH..... THERE SEEMS LITTLE DOUBT ABOUT LIFE AFTER DEATH.

Chapter 33

THE MEANING OF LIFE

After much thought one may conclude that survival is the meaning of life, along with the ability to procreate. However, as we've already discovered life is **IRRELEVANT AND POINTLESS** without **GOD'S LOVE, JOY, AND HOPE**, for these are the **ONLY THINGS** that make life truly worth living.

GOD'S LOVE IS OUR FULFILLMENT, OUR MEANING OF LIFE. FOR WITHIN GOD'S LOVE LIES ALL THE JOY AND HOPE THAT WE NEED TO SURVIVE.

"I can think of no worse punishment, than never knowing the Love of God"

Chapter 34

DEALING WITH DEATH

The human body can't escape death, it's inevitable and can't be prevented. Yet one should not become so overwhelmed by death that their mourning prevents them from sharing and living their life.

This may sound insensitive, especially to those that don't understand death well, but one should never linger with death for too long.

Never forget those that remain with you, life goes on and they will need your love, you must be strong for them.

There is a time to mourn, but study the caterpillar; it's only for a while in its cocoon.

"LIFE AND LOVE IS SUCH THAT IT MUST BE SHARED"

Chapter 35

HAPPINESS

HAPPINESS IS MORE THAN A CHOICE, ONE MUST HAVE A REASON FOR BEING HAPPY.

You may say, I choose to be happy, but you can only trick your mind for a short while before you're asking yourself, WHAT AM I HAPPY ABOUT?

If God's love isn't at the top of your list of things to be most thankful for, your happiness will be artificial and short lived.

If happiness was merely a choice wouldn't we all be happy? However, happiness requires a lot of understanding, forgivingness, patience, trust, and love.

Choosing to be happy is a good start, BUT YOU MUST HAVE A REASON FOR BEING HAPPY, LET GOD BE YOUR REASON !

Chapter 36

CHILDREN BEWARE

Children please remember as you grow older you'll rarely find anything more haunting than REGRET.

"Regret is a terrible prison, one that we ourselves build, and the time we serve can be for a lifetime"

Here is a list of traps that you should be careful not to get caught in:

Don't be a bully; you'll only end up disgracing yourself and your family. There is no honor in picking on the weak.

Don't go along with the crowd just to appear cool. The kids that may seem cool now, the ones that are doing drugs or the ones that are always in trouble, they'll probably be the same ones that can't find their way in life.

Don't be a cutter, or one that harms themselves, it's no way of showing God your love or thankfulness. If you have a compulsion to harm yourself, seek the help of someone you trust, parents, teachers, doctors. Any habit can easily become a compulsion, so it's best to never start. Remember, idle hands can be dangerous, so **SPREAD GODS LOVE.**

Don't be afraid to say **NO** when something isn't right.

Don't allow yourself to be talked into doing foolish things, you'll only end up becoming someone's fool.

Avoid **ANYTHING** having to do with the occult, whether it's for fun or a serious endeavor. Nothing positive will ever come from the darkness. This includes astrology, numerology, readings, ect.

If you're dealing with a problem, don't be afraid to talk to someone that you know is honorable. **DON'T KEEP IT IN!**

PLEASE DON'T USE DRUGS, including marijuana, cigarettes, and alcohol, they're all **VERY HABIT FORMING** or worse. The brain's that these products will alter your thought process. They are also expensive, and nothing good can come from them. "Medical marijuana would be an exception"

If you need to relax, go hiking or fishing, learn to play an instrument, do something creative that makes you feel good. You'll find this type of stimulation is much better than any artificial high.

The damage of drugs are all around you, peer pressure and drugs don't mix, your brain will thank you for it later!

Don't pretend that you know it all, everyone else knows you don't, so don't prove them right. One of the most honest answers you'll ever give is; **I DON'T KNOW,** you'll simply be amazed at the people that will love your honesty.

Don't get the reputation of being a complainer, their gravity brings everyone down.

Don't be cruel to ANYONE, and be kind to EVERYONE.

Don't give in to doing silly pranks, especially ones that could possibly embarrass or hurt someone's feelings. REMEMBER THE GOLDEN RULE.

Post nothing on multi-media that could be an embarrassment to you later. Remember to think twice, and then DON'T.

There are some companies and schools that are currently researching the multi-media history of potential employees and students before hiring or accepting them. In the future it'll become common practice, so be very careful what you post.

Don't liter, and always put your shopping cart away, don't just leave it at your vehicle. Always be respectful to others and set a good example, it shows character.

Don't spread gossip, even if it's true it will never end well for you. Gossip will cost you friendships and no one will ever trust you to keep your mouth shut.

If you must borrow something, bring it back clean and if possible in better condition.

DON'T LIE; IF YOU SAY YOU'RE GOING TO DO SOMETHING, DO IT, YOUR HONOR DEPENDS ON IT! "Your word either has meaning or it doesn't"

Don't forget your manners, **PLEASE, THANK YOU, YOU'RE WELCOME, AND SMILE.**

Don't hold grudges, they'll eat you up. If you want forgiveness, you must learn to give forgiveness.

Don't let yourself go, stay fit and clean. You'll be surprised how much better you'll feel about yourself.

Marriage: If you must live with your parents, then you're not ready for marriage. If you can't afford a place to live, food to eat, money to pay **ALL** your bills, you're not ready. In addition, you're definitely not ready to have children.

When you become 18 you must decide whether you're going to work, trade school, or college. **THE KEY IS TO FIND SOMETHING THAT YOU ENJOY DOING**, and then get the proper training.

Your success and failures are part of the learning process, as such you're 100% responsible for your actions.

Don't play the BLAME GAME.

Making bad choices is a fool's excuse.

Keep in mind, there will be some people that don't like you, "without any reason" so don't sweat it, it's their demon not yours.

Young parents never shake your child, it can be fatal. If you can't handle a crying baby, you must understand that you're not capable of parenting, seek help ASAP.

Parents love your children like you'll never see them again. Also forget that spare the rod or spoil the child nonsense. Research has proven repeatedly it doesn't work.

Researchers at the University of Texas did a meta analysis of 50 years of research on spanking.

The study confirmed that the more children are spanked, the more of a chance of them defying their parents and increasing their anti-social behavior and aggression.

It was also found to impact a child's mental health and cause cognitive difficulties.

In addition, the American Academy of Pediatrics (AAP) does not endorse spanking under any circumstance. It's a form of punishment that becomes less effective with repeated use, according to the AAP; it also makes discipline more difficult as the child outgrows it.

"Spankings instill fear rather than understanding"

Some are going to say "I was spanked as a child and it never hurt me" well maybe it didn't and maybe it did in ways you weren't aware of as a child, such as anxiety and aggression. All children aren't the same, as some may tolerate fear and hitting better than others.

Parents seem to prefer spankings because it's just easier to administer than **TRUE PARENTING**. True parenting takes time, understanding, lots of patience, and lots of love, in other words it requires much more from the parent.

Because spankings are traditional, most parents lack the proper training as they themselves were spanked. As a rule of thumb when it comes to discipline, new parents will follow the example set down by their parents, and their grandparents, and this cycle continues.

It's time that we start parenting with love, and advance beyond this ancient tradition.

Chapter 37

A WORLD WITHOUT RELIGION

Imagine a world without religion, a world where no one pretends to speak on God's behalf, and where everyone understands the importance of uniting as one in Gods infinite love and peace.

A world where there's no divisions, no Christians, no Muslims, Buddhist, Hindus, etc. and **NONE OF THEIR TRADITIONS.**

Imagine a world where churches actually shelter the homeless, and feed the poor. Where the Vatican becomes obsolete and its **BILLIONS** are used to feed the hungry and treat the sick.

> "The Catholic church is the biggest financial power, wealth accumulator and property owner in existence. She is a greater possessor of material riches than any other single institution, corporation, bank, giant trust, government or state of the whole globe" (humansarefree.com)

The Catholic Church isn't about divinity, that's the myth, it's about big business.

THE CATHOLIC CHURCH IS A PERFECT EXAMPLE OF TRUTH BLINDNESS.

OF THESE WHICH IS MORE GODLY AND HOW SHALL YOU ANSWER GOD?

Should you give God one tenth of all your earnings, then hand it over to the Vatican, or a millionaire ministry so they can fuel their private jet or pay the pool person and landscaper to look after their mansion. Or would your tithing be put to better use at a homeless shelter, soup kitchen, or maybe just someone you know that may need help?

Is this truth about tithing not straightforward enough? God doesn't need your money, but if you're in a position to help others, share your blessings.

Going to church isn't a social event, and making the church and the church leaders rich isn't the intention either.

There are those in the clergy that live a modest life and try to help others as best they can, howbeit they are far and few.

In addition, church leaders need not speak on God's behalf. Have we become so ignorant that we can no longer discern the difference between right and wrong, good or evil?

Let the church become a beacon of hope for the community, with their doors always open.

Let the ministers see to the needs of the homeless and hungry, for this is the work of the clergy.

Imagine a world where there's no such thing as jihad, and killing or harming **ANYONE** in the name of God is seen as the evil it truly is, as God plays no part in acts of violence.

If you desire a **TRUE** relationship with God, then you'll need to trust in God, not in religions, traditions or rituals. Don't fear, your spirit will hear God speaking and direct you.

If you seek real change in your life, follow the **TEN COMMANDMENTS**, and put **GOD FIRST** in your life. If your heart is truly sincere, you'll be blessed with more **JOY** and **HOPE** than you can imagine.

NEVER CONFUSE YOUR EGO WITH THE VOICE OF GOD, FOR THE LIST IS LONG WITH THOSE THAT HAVE FALTERED LISTENING TO THE EVILS OF THEIR OWN EGO.

"STAY HUMBLE"

Chapter 38

TRADITIONS AND RITUALS

Religious traditions and rituals are at the very center of Truth Blindness, as these myths are the chains of untruth.

For example; Year after year Christians celebrate Christmas, a holiday with known pagan beginnings, and yet this fact is totally ignored.

Prior to Christmas the Romans celebrated the birthday of Mithra on December 25th. Mithra was known as the god of the unconquerable sun.

Mithra though wasn't the only pagan holiday celebrated during the same period. There was Saturnalia, a holiday in honor of Saturn, the god of agriculture, Juvenalia, a feast honoring the children of Rome, and in Scandinavia, the Norse celebrated Yule from December 21 through January, and the list goes on and on.

Time wise we have no idea about the birth of Jesus, but yet we celebrate his birth every year on December 25th, a day known to have numerous pagan origins.

Why is this day celebrated? **TRADITION**

Why do Christians worship Jesus, a figure that may have never existed? **TRADITION**

Why do Muslims hold tight to their old ways? **TRADITION**

Why does the Catholic Church honor Mary? **TRADITION**

Are we to be evermore imprisoned by traditions that are thousands of year's old, traditions that were brought forth by mystics and rulers of that time?

Since long ago man has identified God, in the image of man.

Why are so many uncomfortable with having an infinite God, preferring God to be in the image of a mere man, thus calling God, HE.

How much longer will you tolerate these ancient myths?

If you are seeking a change in your life, you must let go of these false traditions and rituals.

CHAPTER 39

THOUGHTS AND INSPIRATION

The following is an additional list of some of my own personal thoughts and truths. As they were revealed to me, I share them with you:

Ego is the liar that lurks within us all, the negative side of freewill, also referred to as vanity and Satan.

Well articulated nonsense is often mistaken for truth.

There is no doubt in my mind about the reality of mathematics, but I have never seen an infinite number.

I have little use for defective conversations.

There's power in the Truth.

The fearlessness and foolishness of youth could become your worse regret.

Joy is not found in the abundance of things, but in the magnificence of God's love.

When a shout isn't powerful enough, **WHISPER**.

Regret is a terrible prison, one that we ourselves build, and the time we serve can be for a lifetime.

Conscience and consciousness are both of the body, and therefore can be flawed.

Trying times are often misunderstood blessings.

One shouldn't be too impressed by IQ's, alphabets, or documentation; Its **ORIGINAL** thoughts that are rare.

God's love and wisdom comes with no degree.

When in doubt, always do the right thing.

One must nurture their spirit; recharge it by doing good works, **SPREAD GODS LOVE**.

A child's wonderment is a reminder of what we take for granted.

Making no decision is sometimes the worse decision we can ever make.

There is none richer than the one that possesses God's love.

HELL: An existence without God.

The treasures of God's love, is Joy and Hope.

Honesty is not an excuse for being cruel.

Sometimes it's more important to be kind than correct.

Those that seek forgiveness must give forgiveness.

Emptiness and loneliness is based mostly on INACTIVITY, GET OFF THE PITY WAGON AND GO SPREAD GODS LOVE!

Don't be afraid to show your wings, it's ok to be nice.

Do you love God more than sin?

Never take the short cuts of life. Even though the shortest distance between two points is a straight line, there's no going directly from 1st to 3rd in baseball, or in life.

The truth won't necessarily make you the most popular person in the room.

Life is a series of lessons and no one is excused.

Atheism isn't truth, it's not a fact, and it's not even a good hypothesis. Atheism eliminates possibilities while at the same time minimizing one's existence.

God's love is for everyone.

Faith is knowing that God will help and comfort you through this life.

Don't be like the snake handlers that foolishly put God to the test, for thou shall not tempt the Lord your God.

Everything is within God, as God contains even the universe.

The things of God, are revealed by God.

The following are a few other quotes from various other people you may enjoy:

Life is like riding a bicycle, to keep your balance you must keep moving forward. (Einstein)

Don't play the victim of the consequences you created. (unknown)

Grief is the price of love. (By Dr Colin Murray Parkes)

When you must carry your own water, you learn the value of each drop. (unknown)

Coincidence is God's way of remaining anonymous. (Einstein)

A thing is not necessarily true because a man dies for it. (Oscar Wilde)

"The fanatical atheists are like slaves who are still feeling the weight of their chains which they have thrown off after hard struggle. They are creatures who – in their grudge against traditional religion as the 'opium of the masses' – cannot hear the music of the spheres." (Albert Einstein)

Normal people don't go around destroying others. (Unknown)

Chapter 40

IN CLOSING

As humans, we are imperfect beings, as such we are prone to mistakes, some that we repeat over and over. Because most of our troubles are self-inflicted, it's important that we carefully consider the choices we make.

"Life is a series of lessons and no one is excused"

Because there is more to be learned in trying times, expect trials and tribulations. As you learn to trust in God more and more, you'll find your JOY continues to grow as well.

Also, don't be so hard on yourself, as time passes you'll find it gets easier and easier to control your negative emotions. At 25 you won't be the same person you were in your teens. At 50 you won't be the same person you were when you were 35, etc etc. so hang in there!

REMEMBER TO LIVE WITHIN YOUR MEANS, DEBT DESTROYS FAMILIES.

For those of you that were deceived by the Antichrist, you are lukewarm, return to God. If you thought you were filled with the spirit before, get ready to be blown away with the spirit of God's love!

On a more personal note;

It's only through the grace of God that I'm able to share these truths with you, as I'm just a simple man with my fair share of flaws like anyone else.

For the past 40 years I have studied and researched, feeling compelled and yet constrained to bring these truths into the light. Now that the time is finally here, I pray that God will bless you with the truths found within this book.

ALL GLORY IS GODS, THE ONE AND ONLY LORD AND SAVIOR. A LOVING AND MERCIFUL GOD OF WHICH THERE IS NO OTHER.

LET THE WORD GO OUT: THERE'S NO TRINITY, NO ONE DIED FOR YOUR SINS, NO MEDIATOR IS NECESSARY, NO CRUCIFIXES, ROSARY BEADS, HAIL MARYS, OR ANY OTHER PAGAN NONSENSE IS REQUIRED FROM GOD, THESE ARE All THE INVENTIONS OF MAN-KIND.

SEEK GOD WITH A LOVING AND SINCERE SPIRIT

Blessed are all those whose eyes have been opened, for the TRUTH IS REVEALED ONLY TO THOSE THAT ARE READY.

AMEN

www.ingramcontent.com/pod-product-compliance
Lightning Source LLC
Chambersburg PA
CBHW051924160426

43198CB00012B/2026